CW00833312

The Archaeology of Smoking and Tobacco

The American Experience in Archaeological Perspective

UNIVERSITY PRESS OF FLORIDA

Florida A&M University, Tallahassee
Florida Atlantic University, Boca Raton
Florida Gulf Coast University, Ft. Myers
Florida International University, Miami
Florida State University, Tallahassee
New College of Florida, Sarasota
University of Central Florida, Orlando
University of Florida, Gainesville
University of North Florida, Jacksonville
University of South Florida, Tampa
University of West Florida, Pensacola

The Archaeology of
Smoking and Tobacco

GEORGIA L. FOX

Foreword by Michael S. Nassaney

University Press of Florida

Gainesville · Tallahassee · Tampa · Boca Raton
Pensacola · Orlando · Miami · Jacksonville · Ft. Myers · Sarasota

This book may be available in an electronic edition.

21   20   19   18   17   16   6   5   4   3   2   1

First cloth printing, 2015
First paperback printing, 2016

Library of Congress Cataloging-in-Publication Data
Fox, Georgia Lynne, 1954-
The archaeology of smoking and tobacco / Georgia L. Fox ; foreword by
Michael S. Nassaney.
pages cm. — (American experience in archaeological perspective)
Summary: This book discusses how historical archaeology is well positioned to explore
the role that tobacco and smoking played in the formation of American identities and
cultural practices over a span of three centuries.
Includes bibliographical references and index.
ISBN 978-0-8130-6041-5 (cloth)
ISBN 978-0-8130-5413-1 (pbk.)
1. Tobacco use—United States—History. 2. Smoking—United States—History.
3. Tobacco industry—United States—History. 4. Tobacco—History. 5. Archaeology
and history—United States. I. Nassaney, Michael S. II. Title. III. Series: American
experience in archaeological perspective.
HV5760.F69 2015
362.29'6097—dc23
2014026255

The University Press of Florida is the scholarly publishing agency for the State University
System of Florida, comprising Florida A&M University, Florida Atlantic University,
Florida Gulf Coast University, Florida International University, Florida State University,
New College of Florida, University of Central Florida, University of Florida, University of
North Florida, University of South Florida, and University of West Florida.

University Press of Florida
15 Northwest 15th Street
Gainesville, FL 32611-2079
http://www.upf.com

Contents

Figures

Foreword

As a former smoker, I can clearly recall my adolescent experimentation with tobacco, consciously choosing brands that defined me, and the reluctance to bum a cigarette marketed to women even when I was overcome by desire to smoke. My roll-your-own stage came after I spent a year in Europe that included several visits to Amsterdam, where pouch tobacco and rolling papers were practically obligatory. The ritual and tactile skills that I displayed in producing my hand-rolled cigarettes placed me in the avant-garde among my peers. Years later, I still crave the conviviality of smoking in social settings.

Tobacco use has long been implicated in social and political relations, and for much of its history it left tangible traces that are amenable to archaeological study. Because tobacco's appeal extended to all classes and ethnicities, it provides an entry point into understanding the American experience. White clay smoking pipes are among the most ubiquitous artifacts found on post-Columbian archaeological sites, testifying to the prevalence and longevity of smoking as a cultural practice. Their low-fired earthenware and stone precursors predate imported pipes by hundreds if not thousands of years. In the title of his 1950 book *Tobacco Is American*, Herbert Joseph Spinden left no confusion about its origins. Documentary and archaeological sources demonstrate that tobacco was inextricably woven into the fabric of New World societies when Europeans encountered them beginning in the late fifteenth century. The plant was soon introduced to Europe, where its use was reinterpreted before it diffused to the rest of the Old World and was reintroduced to the Americas. That loathsome weed subsequently became entangled in the formation of American identities and cultural practices; smoking became intertwined with all aspects of social and economic life in America as it came to express class, gender, and ethnic relations.

The ubiquity and embeddedness of tobacco smoking make it ideally amenable to analysis by historical archaeologists who rely on various lines of evidence in their examination of the past, including, of course, documentary sources. Yet it is the materiality of smoking and tobacco use that archaeologists are uniquely suited to decipher. The tangible products of the smoking act provide systematic and quantifiable data on production, distribution, and consumption. In short, most pipes were cheap, disposable, and durable, leading to their frequent preservation and recovery from the archaeological record. They evolved in form to suit the needs of their users and in accordance with shifts in broader markets. Thus pipe bowls increased in size toward the end of the seventeenth century in response to increased availability of tobacco. Even human skeletal remains contain physical traces of smoking behavior in the form of tubercular lesions and dental wear from habitual pipe use. These are concrete manifestations that can be interpreted to provide insights into the identities and contexts of smokers over time and space.

Seldom does an archaeologist investigate a site that does not exhibit some evidence of tobacco use. Tobacco made its way into varied contexts, including saloons, taverns, brothels, forts, battlefields, and mundane sites of work and play. An absence of remains is equally telling. For example, investigations at the mid-nineteenth century home of James and Ellen White in Battle Creek, Michigan, yielded only a few pipe fragments that postdated the Whites' occupancy. This pattern reflects their abhorrence of the pipe—they were, after all, devout Seventh Day Adventists who avoided caffeine, alcohol, meat, and tobacco. This stood in marked contrast with the house lot of their crosstown neighbors, the Shepards, where pipes were common. Warren Shepard was an avowedly middle-class, upwardly mobile Freemason who hired agricultural laborers who were likely responsible for the white clay pipes found immediately outside the attached kitchen to the rear of the house.

In *The Archaeology of Smoking and Tobacco*, Georgia L. Fox examines the roles that tobacco smoking played in the American experience from an archaeological perspective. Her comprehensive summary explores the various lines of evidence that historical archaeologists employ in their studies of tobacco and smoking and highlights a broad range of topics, including chemical residues, skeletal evidence, smoking pipe production techniques, symbolic analysis of design elements, and stylistic change. Fox employs data from numerous case studies to illustrate the geographic and chronological scope of tobacco use from New England and the Chesapeake to the Midwest, the frontier West, and the Caribbean, from the seventeenth through twentieth centuries.

Spatial, temporal, and formal variations in the archaeological record reveal changing American attitudes and beliefs about tobacco from colonial Chesapeake plantations to western saloons, industrial cities, and brothels in our nation's capital. In synthesizing the factors that contributed to the implantation of tobacco production and the ways in which smoking was adopted by different segments of society, Fox provides a valuable contribution to our understanding of the variability and formative role that tobacco and smoking played in North American and North Atlantic history and culture and the archaeological residue that these processes left behind.

Fox begins by situating tobacco alongside other nonessential commodities, while placing it among the earliest such goods in the early modern world. Commodity studies have benefited from analysis at different scales; Fox employs a world-systems framework to highlight the global dynamic that led to tobacco production in the Americas and the accumulation of wealth and social inequality that followed. She rightly notes that the cultivation and trade of tobacco contributed to the development of the institution of slavery in America, thus demonstrating the dramatic and widespread changes that this commodity created. Indeed, enslaved labor made tobacco production possible and changed the course of the American experience forever.

Yet core processes of resource extraction from peripheral areas cannot explain how consumer desire and emulation became expressed in particular consumption patterns. Whereas Native Americans generally used tobacco in ritual contexts, Europeans and others secularized its use and employed it to mark social distinctions in daily life. For example, locally made red clay pipes may have been produced to challenge the monopoly that British pipe makers enjoyed in the seventeenth and eighteenth centuries. While it is not clear who made the red clay forms, their recovery in contexts associated with servants, the poor, and the enslaved suggests that they served to create and maintain socially segregated domestic spaces on Chesapeake plantations. Similarly, the working class at the Lowell textile mills employed shortened pipes, which they could clench between their teeth to free their hands for menial tasks. These "cutties" came to symbolize working-class culture at a time when factory managers and owners had the luxury of enjoying tobacco

in more refined pipes or rolled into expensive cigars. Irish immigrants selected smoking pipes with patriotic designs that served to broadcast their
political leanings. In the course of their class struggles in industrial America,
the Irish were intensifying their ethnicity and making it manifest in outward
symbols, like smoking pipes.

Society has generally been ambivalent about women taking up the pipe,
though this has varied by class, ethnicity, and geography. While public smoking has at times promoted the idea of female promiscuity, moral corruption,
and lack of sexual control, women often challenged these social mores by
engaging in the practice. On the western frontier women were less subject to
societal restrictions: the presence of smoking paraphernalia in places associated with women's activities suggests their indulgence.

The appeal of tobacco goes well beyond mere addiction, despite late twentieth-century understandings about its properties and medical proscriptions
against its use. Fox suggests that its adoption and expansion in the seventeenth century emerged along with desires for other consumable intoxicants
like coffee, alcohol, sugar, and chocolate when income derived from cottage
industries became available to support consumer spending among larger segments of the population. She explains that the persistence of tobacco use
may be sought in the oral pleasure of clutching a pipe between the teeth,
sucking and chewing the stem, and using the mouth in the act of ingestion.
The ritualized acts of packing, tamping, and lighting a bowl and ingesting its
fumes involve an aura of forbidden pleasure that serves as a rite of passage
for some and a moment of solitude or sociability for others. The accoutrements of the smoking ritual—especially pipes—are particularly amenable to
study by historical archaeologists because their morphology and context of
use betray their role as markers of national identity, as they simultaneously
embody values of individuality, independence, freedom of expression, and
patriotism.

Fox has consulted an expansive literature pertaining to the production,
distribution, and consumption of tobacco and smoking pipes and written
an authoritative synthesis on the subject. She argues persuasively that tobacco played a role in every major shift in American life from the fur trade
and revolution to industrialization and civil rights. The mass production of
tobacco is an American phenomenon, and its global marketing is an out-
come of twentieth-century American imperialism. Historical archaeologists

of the future will see white clay pipes as a temporal horizon marker that became eclipsed by cigarettes and their nearly indestructible synthetic filters around the turn of the twentieth century. While cigarette filters have yet to garner any archaeological interest, they are discarded at alarming rates and may lend themselves to understanding the next chapter in the American experience, in which smoking and tobacco persist despite warnings of their hazards. Even as smoking remains controversial and becomes increasingly banned, it betrays attitudes that are deeply seated in the American psyche. The study of tobacco use exposes aspects of the American national character as well as our individual and collective fears and desires.

Michael S. Nassaney
Series Editor

Acknowledgments

Any work is a combination of inspiration, generous support from others, and perseverance through the daily demands of life. In this regard, I would like to acknowledge several important people for their part in the making of this book. I would first like to thank Michael Nassaney of Western Michigan University for encouraging me to go forward with the book in his series as well as for his support in the development of the manuscript. It was his expert guidance that helped make this book a reality. I would also like to thank Frederick Smith and Charles Orser for their helpful and constructive comments on the drafts of the manuscript. I am especially grateful to Fred, whose book *The Archaeology of Alcohol and Drinking* served as a text in my Historical Archaeology course; it was then that I realized the potential for a similar book on tobacco and smoking. Thank you for the inspiration, Fred!

This acknowledgment would be incomplete without recognizing Donny L. Hamilton, who first introduced me to the joys of archaeological discovery and historical archaeology through the Port Royal field school in the summer of 1986. I subsequently did my research on the 21,575 white clay tobacco pipes recovered from Port Royal, Jamaica. Since then, the body of archaeological literature on tobacco and smoking has grown to include several distinguished publications by colleagues. An assemblage of archaeological artifacts remains only that until we are able to delve more deeply into associated meanings that reflect a society in a certain time and place. For this, I also have to thank other mentors like Bruce Dickson and Sylvia Grider, who taught me the rigors and importance of maintaining strong theoretical perspectives in interpreting the material life of the past, whether it be Upper Paleolithic cave art or the expressions of the "folk." I would also like to extend sincere gratitude to the staff at the George Arents Collection in the New

York Public Library, the British Museum, the National Archives Public Record Office, London, and the helpful staff at the California State University (CSU), Chico, Meriam Library Interlibrary Loan unit. I would like to offer heartfelt thanks to my students, who continually inspire me with their lively questions and thought-provoking ideas. Special thanks are due to the editors at the University Press of Florida, particularly Meredith Morris-Babb, for helpful suggestions and guidance along the way. I would like to thank P. Willey for generously contributing his images of dental pathologies and Paul Reckner for his photo of the Five Points pipes. The manuscript has benefited greatly from the keen editorial eye of Stefanie Kline. I thank my colleagues in the Department of Anthropology at CSU Chico, as well as family and friends, for their ongoing support and good cheer during this journey.

1

Introduction

Over 1 billion people smoke tobacco worldwide, making it one of the most widely used and popular drugs in human history. The inclusion of the Surgeon General's Warning on a package of cigarettes, along with well-publicized lawsuits against the major tobacco companies, reminds us of the ill effects of smoking tobacco. Yet contrasting media images often reinforce the notion that smoking is a sophisticated activity, perhaps associated with artistry, creativity, and individuality. From both diachronic and synchronic perspectives, tobacco smoking also presents itself as a highly ritualized event, from Native American ceremonies to Chinese business negotiations.

Despite its global impact, the phenomenon of tobacco has its roots in the Americas, from indigenous use to its introduction to European explorers in the fifteenth century. Tobacco can be considered one of the first true American commodities to enter the colonial export trade (Horn 1994: 6). Proof can be found in the archaeological record. Along with piles of broken and discarded ceramics, corroded nails, and other artifacts, clay tobacco pipes are sprinkled on the trash heaps of historical archaeological sites, testifying to the popularity of smoking. Thus historical archaeology is well suited to reveal the story of tobacco in America.

The main theme of this book is to demonstrate how well positioned historical archaeology is to explore the role that tobacco and smoking played in the formation of American identities and cultural practices over a span of more than three hundred years. As mass consumables, tobacco, sugar, and other stimulants revolutionized the world and changed the course of history. The New World cultivation and export of tobacco fostered the development of social transformations both in Europe and in the colonies. Throughout the subsequent centuries, tobacco smoking in America would come to represent and symbolize deeply held ideas about identity, gender, status, and class, in the relational sense (see Wurst 2006). Tobacco was also instrumental in negotiating politically charged relations between various actors in diverse contexts.

For historical archaeologists, clay tobacco pipes have been primarily used as a relative dating tool. Only recently have clay pipes been subject to more in-depth anthropological investigations for assessing culture change and processes in the Americas. Works by Lauren Cook (1989), Michael Nassaney (2004), Sean Rafferty and Rob Mann (2004), Paul Reckner (2001, 2004), myself (Fox 2004), and others provide meaningful analyses in the interpretation of Native North American ethnohistories, working-class culture in Lowell, Massachusetts, patriotism in New York's Five Points neighborhood, and socioeconomic change in British America.

What does historical archaeology have to offer in the study of tobacco and smoking in the American experience? Historical archaeology can contribute to the dialogue in three ways. First, it is text-aided through the documentary record. One of the great joys of working in the historical period is using primary sources and iconographic evidence that can either refute or support the archaeological evidence as well as testing proposed models and theories. For example, probate inventories and shipping records can shed light on the economies of the colonial tobacco trade as well as the distribution and trade of clay pipes. Pamphlets, tracts, advertisements, and Dutch genre paintings are some of the many sources that can offer insight into the more symbolic aspects of tobacco and its material culture.

Second, historical archaeology offers tangible evidence for the long trajectory of the various economic, social, and cultural contexts in which tobacco use took place, from early culture contact to the more recent past. Long before the arrival of Europeans, indigenous use of tobacco played a key role in Native American relations, spirituality, and cosmology. As part of the "Columbian Exchange," documented European encounters with Native Americans using tobacco began with Christopher Columbus's second voyage in 1493. Not long thereafter, specimen samples of tobacco plants were brought back to Europe for cultivation. With an unprecedented zeal, society transformed tobacco from a "curious" substance of indigenous peoples to an economically important commodity (Heidtke 1992: 117). The archaeological evidence for such developments can be seen in the remains of clay tobacco pipes, which were easy to transport, smoke, and discard. Once clay pipes were mass produced, they became the ubiquitous accessory to daily life, as revealed by the thousands of pipes found on historical sites such as Port Royal, Jamaica (see chapter 6).

Third, historical archaeology is suitable for the study of tobacco because of its focus on exploring the lives of everyday people, the less documented and "voiceless" peoples who were instrumental in forging a nation (Orser 1996: 68). This begins with indigenous peoples, followed by the early English colonists and later immigrants who populated the cities and towns of a growing country. I hope that this study demonstrates that tobacco provides an excellent means by which to understand how various groups formed their identities as they faced the challenges of modernization, globalization, and culture change, as tobacco's appeal extended to all classes and ethnicities.

In the discussion on tobacco and smoking, it is necessary to appreciate the important role that alcohol played, as drinking and smoking often went hand in hand. Alcohol and tobacco were part of the group of drug/stimulant foods that anthropologist Sidney Mintz (1985: 99–100, 1996: 19–20) refers to in *Sweetness and Power* and *Tasting Food, Tasting Freedom*. David Courtwright (2002: 2) refers to alcohol, tobacco, and caffeine as the big three stimulants of the "psychoactive revolution," and it is no coincidence that the rapid growth of distilling, tobacco imports, and coffeehouses all happened within the seventeenth century. Psychoactive substances are a natural fit for anthropological study, because they are a part of the anthropology of consumption (Sherratt 2007: 6). Rather than treat such consumables separately, Phil Withington (2011: 637) suggests that it makes more sense to view alcohol, tobacco, coffee, and other commodities as a group of intoxicants that spanned a wide social spectrum, as they gained popularity in the early modern era.

Having a psychoactive chemical effect on the human brain, tobacco has long served as a drug of choice for inducing altered states of consciousness, especially during Native American rites and ceremonies. Rafferty and Mann (2004: xiii) have described tobacco pipes as "drug delivery devices." For Europeans, tobacco may have been used to curb hunger among the poor and at times for medicinal purposes (Braudel 1979: 261; Brooks 1937, 1: 31; Goodman 1993: 43; Monardes [1577] 1925: 90; Shammas 1990: 297).

Some scholars attribute the appeal of tobacco to its addictive qualities; yet the use of tobacco cannot be fully explained by addiction alone. In fact, Janet Farrell Brodie and Marc Redfield (2002: 4) argue that the concept of addiction itself is essentially a modern and predominantly Western cultural construct. The concept of addiction, born of the late Victorian age, reflected an emerging risk-taking society, whereby a confluence of industrialization, urbanization, consumerism, and affluence intersected with individual freedom of choice and autonomy. This took place against a social backdrop of self-control; anyone who deviated from this (say, in terms of excessive behavior) was deemed by the medical profession to be pathological, suffering from a disease of the will. An individual's overpowering desire for substances like alcohol and opium became known as addiction. Such behavior was seen not only as a medical disease but also as a moral failing that posed a threat to the stable order of society. This became a paradox of modern life—the freedom to choose—where the individual risked the very real possibility of becoming enslaved or victimized by the act of conscious choice (Lyng 2005: 12; Margolis 2002: 20; Reith 2004: 283–84, 287–88). In this respect, the idea of addiction thus became "a radical break from the past," as a condition of modernity and an industrialized capitalist society where opiates, alcohol, tobacco, and other substances were available for any consumer who could afford or obtain them (Alexander and Roberts 2003: 2; Brodie and Redfield 2002: 3).

Despite its addictive qualities, tobacco smoking functioned in two main capacities: to provide solace and as a form of sociability. As a drug, like alcohol, tobacco could alleviate anxiety resulting from the unpredictability of life (Smith 2008: 99). Given the tensions sparked by European and indigenous encounters, the fear and uncertainty of colonial settlement, and the encroaching complexities of modern life with the rise of capitalism and the Industrial Revolution, the adoption of tobacco in the last several hundred years makes sense as a salve to help ease social tensions.

People also enjoyed tobacco for pure pleasure and sociability, however, as they did with alcohol. Both were often consumed in public places and in an atmosphere of conviviality. The appearance of clay pipes in the archaeological record may reflect these behaviors and provides a window into the social transformations that occurred over the course of American history. The wholesale adoption of tobacco smoking and usage ushered in new habits that became deeply ingrained in the culture. Tobacco smoking engendered the material objects of smoking, such as clay tobacco pipes, tobacco boxes, and other accoutrements, and most importantly signaled the beginning of an early consumerism and the desire for non-necessities made possible by changing socioeconomic conditions. Such conditions were stimulated through expanding markets in a developing system of trade and colonization and the importation of raw materials that could be processed into readily consumable goods like tobacco, coffee, sugar, and other commodities that became available in the early modern era.

More than a century later, social life came to represent group and personal identity formations that could be expressed through the act of tobacco smoking itself, its material culture, and related activities, both public and private (see chapter 5). Such social transformations were important, because they mirrored the broader American national identity, which was perceived as including qualities of individuality, freedom of expression, and pride in a country often characterized by ambition and restlessness in its growth and development.

Chapter Overviews

To situate the reader, chapter 2 delves into several theoretical constructs that offer a means by which to understand the popularity of tobacco and smoking. They include world-systems analysis and consumer theory, which dovetail, while requiring some modifications. The world-systems analysis of Immanuel Wallerstein (1974, 1980) and André Gunder Frank (1978) serves as a useful theoretical tool to study the roots of a precapitalistic society in historical archaeology; but as in the case of many theoretical frameworks, one size does not fit all. The model overlooks the role of desire in influencing consumer choice in the early modern era. Although Wallerstein (1974: 302) recognized that non-necessities (which he called "preciosities") represented a specialized trade in the world-systems exchange between core and periphery, the element of desire helped instigate the agricultural initiatives of tobacco and sugar cultivation. This book proposes that the *desire* for luxury goods and psychoactive consumables such as tobacco provided the bridge between the world-systems model and the growth of mass consumption in a preindustrial era.

Consumerism and consumer theory also offer historical archaeologists a number of ways to explain consumer choice and aspects of desire. For example, tobacco clay pipes were used to express identities and affiliations among Irish immigrants and working-class laborers. Yet smoking tobacco was not fully embraced by all members of society: it remained a forbidden pleasure for middle-class and upper-class Victorian women, who often smoked in secret. The foundation for the consumption of tobacco is explored in chapter 3, which covers the adoption of tobacco and smoking, beginning with the indigenous roots of tobacco use and its "discovery" and appropriation by Europeans in the sixteenth century. Developments in the Chesapeake tobacco economy are explored, particularly in relation to the introduction of slavery that made the tobacco economy possible.

Chapter 4 discusses the material world of smoking, especially in regard to the archaeological remains of tobacco clay pipes, perhaps one of the most common artifacts encountered by historical archaeologists. Chapter 5 concerns the role of tobacco and smoking in the formation of American life. Using case studies in historical archaeology, this chapter examines various aspects of tobacco use throughout North America. Chapter 6 presents the case of Port Royal, Jamaica, where smoking became an integral part of English culture and society in both the New and Old Worlds. Chapter 7 concludes the study.

The recent focus on tobacco as a line of inquiry in historical archaeology expands on a growing body of literature in anthropology, material culture studies, and American Studies. Taking a body of data (such as clay pipes), the study of tobacco and its material culture provides new avenues for examining cultural change through time. The study of consumer preference and material culture in America has been well documented through much inspired scholarship, including Jane Perkins Claney's study of Rockingham Ware (2004) and Frederick Smith's study of the material culture of alcohol and drinking (2008). Analyzing and interpreting these rich bodies of data allows researchers to "read" the artifacts as reflections of the cultures and societies that created and appropriated them. Clay tobacco pipes as artifacts can be read as objects that embody people's attitudes and beliefs as part of the American experience. The chapters in this book explore tobacco usage from various vantage points, with case studies derived from Port Royal, Jamaica, and North America. The transformations that occurred in over three hundred years of New World cultures and societies can be traced through the ubiquitous and humble clay pipe, a mass-produced commodity that hinted at things to come.

2

Theoretical Approaches to Studying Tobacco and Smoking in Historical Archaeology

Once tobacco is smoked, chewed, or inhaled—like any food-related substance—it vanishes, often replaced by the desire for more. Tobacco's ephemeral nature and use as a consumer good made it one of the first nonessential commodities in the history of the early modern world. To explain tobacco's role in four centuries of cultural and economic transformations, this book employs two theoretical approaches to the study of tobacco in historical archaeology: world-systems analysis and consumer theory. Both of these theoretical perspectives are suited to this particular study. As historical archaeology is multiscalar, world-systems theory and consumer theory allow for a macro-view, while consumer theory on a micro-scale accommodates human action and agency to explain culture change in the unfolding of modernity (Hall and Silliman 2006: 9).

World-Systems Analysis

World-systems analysis or theory, inspired by Fernand Braudel and proposed by Immanuel Wallerstein and André Gunder Frank, provides a useful framework for historical archaeologists working in the early modern period, because it allows for the study of culture change on a broad scale (Braudel 1979; Lucas 2006: 39). Wallerstein first introduced world-systems analysis (also referred to as "dependency theory") in 1974 in his seminal book *The Modern World System*. As a social scientist, Wallerstein's goal has been to create a constructive means by which to examine and analyze world history and social change through a multidisciplinary macro-scale approach. As a scholar of postcolonial Africa, Wallerstein has been interested in how relationships of dependency resulted from the *longue durée* of an emerging capitalist world economy and industrialization, beginning with developments in the sixteenth century. André Gunder Frank's work on colonialism in Latin America (1978) has also played an integral role in the creation of the world-systems model.

The rise of British hegemony through colonization and trade offers an exceptional example of world-systems theory in action. Applying Wallerstein's model to British America, the system is characterized by a set of mechanisms that redistribute resources such as raw materials from the *periphery* (in this case the New World colonies) to the *core*, the center of power (London and later Bristol, as more than one economic core can exist simultaneously) (Braudel 1977: 81–82). In this scenario, peripheral areas are divided into two zones: the semiperipheral or middle zone, characterized by some attributes of both the core and the periphery but often exploited by the core powers; and the larger outlying peripheral areas, typified by labor-intensive production and simple technologies (Eisenmenger and Giljum 2007: 293).

For example, in the core-periphery relationship, the Chesapeake and Caribbean colonies grew the tobacco, providing London with barrels full of raw unprocessed tobacco leaves. The tobacco was culled and prepared for smoking and then re-exported and distributed back to the colonies and elsewhere to be enjoyed by the burgeoning population of smokers. In turn for providing the raw tobacco product, the colonies relied on and received manufactured goods, such as building materials, furniture, tools, and foodstuffs produced in Britain's core manufacturing areas. Such goods enabled colonists to establish and sustain their settlements and to create a level of comfort for those living in uncertain and often anxiety-ridden circumstances. London, as the nucleus of operations, relied on the Crown and a variety of investors to make shrewd business decisions predicated on London's economic, social, and political capital (Abel 2007: 56).

The world-systems model also includes the semiperiphery, those entities that bridged the core and periphery. In the case of tobacco, the semiperiphery between London and the tobacco-producing New World colonies would include important port cities and hubs like Boston, New York, and Philadelphia. These semiperipheral entities provided access to goods and key players involved in the maritime trade, thus oiling the wheels of commerce between London and, say, Barbados. Researchers like Gil Stein (1999: 18) question whether semiperipheral areas actually acted as stabilizing buffers between core and periphery. But they provided the much-needed contacts and markets for the British colonies until unforeseen circumstances such as war and related embargos and blockades disrupted the flow. For a time, the system was well orchestrated but was indeed subject to fluctuations, interruptions, and unexpected turns of events.

As a theoretical approach, world-systems theory has proved to be suitable for analyzing events and outcomes from an anthropological perspective, but it has received criticism on a number of fronts. Chief among dissenting opinions is the argument that colonization was not central to England's economic development. This claim is based on the idea that colonial trade was insufficient to warrant any significant source of capital. Therefore colonial markets were simply too small to induce any real kind of industrial development in core areas like London (O'Brien 1982; McCusker and Menard 1991: 44).

In some instances this argument is valid. Yet in the case of tobacco the benefits outweighed the disadvantages. A closer look at the latter part of the seventeenth century reveals a thriving overseas trade for England; the integrated system of trade between Europe and its colonies in the eighteenth century could be regarded as one of the first "global" markets of the Atlantic world (Hancock 2000: 106). This market was fueled by the introduction of tobacco as a marketable commodity from the Chesapeake and Caribbean colonies. In fact, agricultural products like sugar and tobacco stimulated England's economy. By the early 1770s, American agricultural exports to Britain accounted for 40 percent of the overseas commerce, with the colonies importing another 40 percent of British manufactured goods (Price 1978: 122–23; Nash 1999: 95, 98; McCusker 1997: 314). This was further enhanced by employing British laborers to process the raw materials imported from the colonies (Price 1978: 123).

Another criticism leveled at world-systems theory has been the absence of "voiceless" indigenous peoples and individuals in the periphery, who were as much a part of the historical processes as those holding the reins of power (Wolf 1982; Stein 1999: 19). In terms of the trajectory of tobacco, this accounts for a significant sector of participants and actors in the adoption of tobacco and smoking, particularly Africans and Native Americans.

Recent scholars have proposed that other agents influenced the world-systems exchange, including geopolitical and military factors, gender roles and relations, communications, urban growth and cosmopolitanism, and the growing importance of luxury and prestige goods (Chase-Dunn and Hall 1997: 13, 59; Hall 2000; Hughs 2012; Fox 2004: 87–88). Wallerstein includes "bulk" goods in his formulations, which were necessary for the colonies to sustain their existence, particularly at the outset. Yet world-systems theory misses the mark in that luxury goods and nonessentials (like tobacco clay pipes, for example) figured prominently in the colonial trade. Although Wallerstein (1974: 302) recognized that specialized trade existed in what he termed "preciosities" (items not required for survival), he overlooked the rise of preindustrial consumer *demand* for luxury goods. For many historical archaeologists, thousands of artifacts and documentation in the form of colonial probate inventories and shipping records provide compelling evidence to support this. Human nature functions as a potent motivator for spending to acquire anything from tobacco to Chinese porcelain. Recent scholarship by Carole Shammas (1990, 2000), Lorna Weatherill (1988), and others challenges the commonly held assumption that the "consumer revolution" did not begin until the Industrial Revolution. The rapid acceptance of tobacco provides a robust example of active preindustrial consumer behavior. Although smokers may disagree, tobacco was not a necessity in the seventeenth century or today.

In *Capitalism and Material Life, 1400–1800*, Fernand Braudel (1973: 188) observes that stimulant foods like tea, coffee, sugar, and chocolate enlivened the monotony of daily life, where "every civilization needs dietary luxuries and stimulants." The craze for pepper and spices in Western Europe in the twelfth and thirteenth centuries is a prime example, followed by alcohol in the sixteenth century, and then "tea and coffee, not to mention tobacco" (Braudel 1973: 188). As Sidney Mintz notes (1996: 19), the desire for these stimulants developed during overseas expansion and colonial conquest. Colonization became the golden goose of economic initiatives that would secure overseas markets, revenues from taxed goods, and the production of specialized commodities (Frank 1978: 65; Wallerstein 1980: 7). Until the full-scale adoption of sugar as the predominant monocrop in the Americas, tobacco was the most remunerative crop in early colonization efforts by the English, particularly in the Caribbean and Chesapeake (Menard 1980: 151; Nash 1999: 95). Simply put, the desire for tobacco helped fuel the developing world system of colonization and trade.

David Hancock (2000: 106–7) maintains that tobacco ideally exemplifies the "hub and spoke" nature of dependency theory. As an agricultural commodity, the import/export trade of tobacco was both financed and managed by various investors, sea captains, and merchants who shipped and processed the raw tobacco leaves then re-exported processed tobacco back to the colonies. These activities involved an ever-expanding range of brokers in London, Glasgow, Bristol, Liverpool, and Whitehaven. The enforcement of the restrictions established by the English Navigation Acts in order to protect against foreign competition also ensured continued dominance of London and Bristol over the colonial periphery (Hancock 2000: 106–7).

As Russell Menard (2007: 310) asserts, before the passage of the first Navigation Act in 1651, English initiatives in America had consisted of "an informal association, bound together by the subordination of the several colonies to the Crown, by the common culture and identities of the colonists, and most importantly, by the activities of London merchants who linked the relatively distinct enterprises around the Atlantic from New England to the Caribbean into a more or less coherent commercial whole." The English Navigation Acts thus provided a formal structure to protect English interests and investments in agricultural commodities like sugar and tobacco, which were essential for establishing the foundation of a developing world system. The desire for such commodities assured Britain's eventual place front and center on the world stage, with the most formidable navy and hegemonic power to defend its capital investments worldwide.

Consumer Theory

The culture of tobacco and smoking began as a novelty, a luxury product that quickly morphed into a popular nonessential: affordable for most, easily accessible, and in high demand. If tobacco was and still is desired as a non-necessity, what has been its long-term appeal as a consumer good? For historical archaeologists, one of the ways to approach this question is to consider consumption theory as an explanation for historical developments from the sixteenth through early twentieth centuries.

Two mechanisms of consumer demand, emulation and desire, provide a way of "closing the gap" that world-systems theory creates in explaining the popularity of consumer goods. The "trickle down" theory of Thorstein Veblen, as presented in his pioneering work *The Theory of the Leisure Class* (1899), is not always appropriate to explain certain aspects of consumer behavior. But in the case of tobacco it makes sense, at least for the early adoption of tobacco in the seventeenth and eighteenth centuries. As Paul Mullins (2011: 42–43) observes, the problem with the Veblen model is its excellence in explaining the mechanisms of emulation and desire but its failure to explain the *why* of a commodity's appeal. This essentially removes consumers from the power of their personal choices and agency to act in their own behalf. In examining tobacco and smoking, a more well-rounded approach would be to include both the external forces (like wages and prices) acting on individual agency and aspects of personal choice.

Although emulation and desire are useful models in probing consumer behavior for the early modern period, they are not as effective for determining the mass appeal of tobacco and smoking for the nineteenth and early twentieth centuries as they relate to the American experience. For the purposes of this study, a more suitable method is to investigate consumer behavior through politics and identity. To avoid the trap of essentialism, where consumer choice is dictated by the objective historical factors that influence people's lives, including culture and geography, a more nuanced approach would be to examine those factors as well as "how people actively define themselves and others" (Mullins 2011: 115). This poses its own challenges, as archaeologists are aware of the pitfalls of trying to identify ethnic markers in the archaeological record.

As Mullins (2011: 2–3) reflects, consumption is a complex area of research for historical archaeologists, whereby they are "compelled to wrestle with somewhat messy dimensions of desire, identity fluidity, and symbolic multivalence." From Pierre Bourdieu's *Distinction* (1984) to Jacques Maquet's *Aesthetic Experience* (1988), consumer behavior can be viewed from a number of perspectives useful to anthropologists, but each construction has its advantages and disadvantages. For example, in studying such a seemingly simple act as smoking a pipe, the archaeologist may adopt Bourdieu's approach, explaining the nondiscursive knowledge and experiences of certain groups and individuals as to why they smoked but ignoring their internalized and complex and sometimes contradictory sensibilities. As Mullins (2011: 2–3) aptly points out, we cannot reduce material symbolism to explicit notions of human identities and assign rational coherence where it may not exist. Consumer behavior itself is not always rational.

The challenges are real for historical archaeologists, but the archaeological record does offer some level of consistency, providing a body of artifacts to research and analyze, the opportunity to consult historical records, and a rich treasure trove of imagery, not to mention oral histories. In sum, rather than attempt to impose one unifying theory of consumption as it relates to tobacco and smoking, a far more cogent study is created by visualizing tobacco and smoking as a form of consumption, but from different approaches within consumption theory. The simple clay smoking tobacco pipe provides an illustration of this. The mass production of these mold-produced pipes as early as the seventeenth century not only reveals the desire to consume tobacco but reflects the throw-away nature of the pipes, both locally made and imported. This resulted in the sizable amounts of clay pipes found on archaeological sites worldwide, particularly in such New World colonies as Port Royal, Jamaica, where thousands of pipes were recovered in ten years of excavation. Without the desire for tobacco and its consumption, the archaeological record would most likely be deficient in clay tobacco pipe remains; because they were produced, distributed, and used in vast quantities, however, they serve as a testament to tobacco's popularity as a highly desired commodity.

Tobacco and smoking in seventeenth-century Port Royal, Jamaica, offers an excellent case study for examining aspects of desire and emulation (see chapter 6). But tobacco and smoking in both urban and rural contexts in American history can be more thoroughly investigated and more fully appreciated through a focus on identity formation and politics from early colonization to more recent times (see chapter 5). From Irish laborers to soldiers on the American frontier, this aspect of consumer theory provides historical archaeologists with the paths to pursue the in-depth study of the cultural codes of various groups as well as the deeper meanings in tobacco consumption and the material culture of smoking. Thus artifacts of the recent past can speak volumes about the people who made and used them. Centuries of silence are broken through the power of the pipe, revealing the hopes, desires, and the existence of the "folk," with narratives unpacked and loaded with meaning.

Conclusion

By utilizing world-systems analysis and consumption theory, historical archaeologists can probe the mechanisms of culture change as they relate to the adoption of tobacco. World-systems theory illustrates the complex dependencies between the centers of power and colonial peripheries in the early modern era, tracing how and when they developed. Through the agricultural initiatives of early planters in the Chesapeake and Caribbean colonies, as well as enterprising investors and middlemen, tobacco became one of the first major agricultural commodities in the developing world system of transatlantic markets and trade. Raw materials were imported from the colonies, refined, then re-exported and taxed as nonessential goods.

None of this could be possible without consumer demand and the desire for the broad-leafed weed, which gained popularity with a zeal previously unknown in human history. Close on its heels was the demand for sugar, signifying burgeoning interests in new taste sensations and prompting changes in human preferences and habits. Where world-systems theory falls short is in its omission of human desire, a vital link to the creation and sustenance of markets. This is where consumption theory can fill in the gaps, through not only its capacity to account for human desire but also its ability to expand the broad spectrum of individual and group identities, within shifting and changing contexts. Currency and capital might make the world go round, but human desire and choice help stoke the fires of change, as human cultures and societies adapt and adjust to their present-day realities and anticipate their futures. In this regard, historical archaeology is well poised to address both great and small changes over time, through the study and analysis of tobacco and smoking, as illustrated in the following chapters.

3

That Loathsome Weed

The Adoption of Tobacco and Smoking

Many historical archaeologists can testify to the ubiquity of clay tobacco smoking pipes, whether Dutch, English, American, or locally made. Spectacular amounts have been recovered from the archaeological record. The collection at Colonial Jamestown, containing stem and bowl fragments, includes well over 50,000 pipes dating from 1620 to 1690 (Cotter 1994). At Port Royal, Jamaica, 21,575 English clay pipes were recovered in ten years of excavation (Fox 1999: 1). The seventeenth-century "Pipe Wreck," located at Monti Christi, Dominican Republic, yielded about 25,000 Dutch clay pipes (Hall 1996: 118). Smaller but still substantial amounts (over 2,000) were tallied for the Green Spring Plantation, Virginia (Crass 1988), the Chaney's Hills Site in Maryland (Callage, Kille, and Luckenbach 1999), and the Fort Union Trading Post in North Dakota (Sudbury 2009).

What do these clay pipe remains mean to the historical archaeologist? A closer look at the body of evidence reveals a fascinating history of the adoption and wide-scale use of tobacco and smoking. Two New World plants dominate the narrative: *Nicotiana tabacum* and *Nicotiana rustica. N. tabacum* is a pink-flowered species that was primarily grown in Mexico, Central and South America, and the Caribbean region and then transplanted in the Chesapeake region. *N. rustica*, a yellow-flowered species from the North American mainland, was adopted on a more limited basis (figures 1 and 2). Both forms had their own particular characteristics to the discerning smoker. *N. rustica*, with its higher nicotine content, had more psychotropic properties, whereas *N. tabacum* was deemed milder to the palate (Turnbaugh 1975: 66; Winter 2000a: 99).

Figure 1. Illustration of *Nicotiana tabacum* by Nicolas Jose Rapún. "Instruccion General de el Cultivo de Tavacos" (1764).

Figure 2. Illustration of *Nicotiana rustica* by O. C. Berg and C. F. Schmidt. *Darstellung und Beschreibung sämmtlicher in der Pharmacopoea Borussica aufgeführten offizinellen Gewächse, etc.* (1858–1863).

Tobacco was used in many forms by indigenous peoples throughout the Americas: it was rolled in cigar-like fashion, smoked in pipes, and chewed. In Antelope Cave in Arizona, archaeologists recovered tobacco quids or "balls," dating to the Basketmaker III Period (A.D. 400–800). These quids consisted of tobacco bits and other materials intertwined among yucca fibers and were chewed, releasing the potent effects of *N. rustica* (Keith Johnson, personal communication, September 13, 2013). As fairly strong stuff, the higher nicotine content of *N. rustica* conferred a marked advantage for Native Americans seeking alternate states of consciousness in vision quests and in shamanistic rites and ceremonies involving communication with the spirit world (von Gernet 1995: 68). Overall, the cultivation and use of tobacco in the Americas goes hand in hand with the evolution of Indian religious and sociopolitical organization (Winter 2000a: 99, 2000c: 265). Cultivation of tobacco may have preceded the domestication of food crops, with plant selections based on achieving favored psychotropic effects (Winter 2000b: 326).

According to Jordan Goodman (1993), the appropriation of tobacco by Europeans occurred along two possible trajectories. The first was the sharing of tobacco between Native Americans and European explorers, and the other resulted from an "intellectual assimilation" of tobacco from the New World into European cultures in a complete cycle of adoption and exchange across the Atlantic. Written records may have facilitated this process, with documents ranging from explorers' accounts to advertisements or tracts and pamphlets (Goodman 1993: 47; Mancall 2004).

The religious use of sacred tobacco by indigenous peoples stood in stark contrast to the discovery and recreational use of tobacco by sailors on Columbus's first voyage to Hispaniola in 1492 (Winter et al. 2000: 358). Most accounts acknowledge Columbus as having recorded the first reference to tobacco. Anchored off the coast of Cuba, he wrote in his diary entry for November 6: "My two men met many people crossing their path to reach their villages, men and women, carrying in their hand a burning brand and herbs, which they used to produce fragrant smoke" (Columbus [1492] 1992: 115). The men and women were indigenous Taínos, who utilized tobacco by smoking it in a cigar-like form.

In 1499 Amerigo Vespucci observed indigenous peoples chewing tobacco on the island of Margarita off the coast of Venezuela (Brooks 1937, 1: 19). In

1535 the French explorer Jacques Cartier witnessed pipe smoking by Native Americans living along the St. Lawrence River (Poling 2012: 24–25). Other Europeans, notably Spanish and Portuguese explorers, encountered tobacco in a variety of situations. The earliest published account of tobacco use is attributed to the Spanish viceroy Gonzalo Fernández de Oviedo y Valdés, while living in the Spanish colonies. In his *Historia General y Natural de las Indias*, first published in 1526, Oviedo observed that tobacco was inhaled by inserting the ends of a fork-shaped tube that the Indians called a *tabaco* into the nostrils, with the burning leaves placed in the single end of the tube (Brooks 1937, 1: 204; Fairholt 1859: 14).

Oviedo refers to this as "drinking" the smoke, although what he probably witnessed was the inhalation of snuff, which he confused with smoking rolled tobacco (Brooks 1937, 1: 202; Mackenzie 1958: 64). The term *tabaco* was applied to the name of the forked tube that Oviedo mentions in his account, although Bartolomé de Las Casas while on Hispaniola also reported that Taíno Indians smoked rolled tobacco called *tabacos*. Perhaps the most influential encounters occurred in the southeastern United States, in Florida and Virginia, where Europeans met indigenous peoples smoking small pipes. Their shapes most likely served as prototypes in the development of European clay pipes. For example, English sailors under the command of Sir John Hawkins in 1565 observed the local Florida Indians smoking tobacco through a small pipe that consisted of a "cane and an earthen cup in the end" (Hakluyt 1904: 57).

The expedition of Sir Walter Raleigh and Thomas Hariot to Virginia Colony in 1585 was perhaps one of the most seminal moments in the introduction of tobacco to Europeans (see Hariot [1590] 1972). Hariot's role was to provide a scientific assessment of the territory and economic potential (Noël Hume 1994: 29). In the course of recording detailed observations, Hariot learned about tobacco cultivation and smoking from the local Algonquian Indians, all of which he published in *A Briefe and True Report of the New Found Land of Virginia* (1590). In this case, the indigenous method involved using either a tubular pipe or an elbow pipe. Both Hariot and Raleigh were credited with introducing tobacco to England upon their return.

Following these early encounters, explorers carried tobacco seeds back to Europe, which provided the main stock for future plants. By 1570 much of Europe had been exposed to tobacco. Tobacco made its way into Asia,

India, and West Africa beginning in the early 1600s, and commercial culti-vation of *N. tabacum* had been established both in England and in the New World colonies (Brooks 1937, 1: 42; Goodman 1993: 37). Ironically, as Joseph Winter et al. (2000: 360) observe, the more accessible and easily imported *N. tabacum* not only became the tobacco preferred by Native Americans with the establishment of the fur trade in the mid-1600s but also served as a substitute for local traditional varieties in indigenous ceremonial life. In essence, *N. tabacum* became a commodity of dependency in trade relations between Europeans and Native Americans.

Tobacco and England's Economic Recovery

Although little was known about tobacco at the time of its "discovery," this potent leaf held great promise for future prosperity along with the capacity to instigate dramatic and sweeping changes that would resonate powerfully for generations, particularly in the American colonies. Like sugar, tobacco changed the world significantly by impacting and transforming well-estab-lished customs and cultural traditions, spending and consumer habits, pop-ulation demography, land use, and human relations. A good case in point is Great Britain, with its rise from a largely agrarian society to a goliath empire. This power can be attributed in part to an economic recovery accomplished through a number of initiatives. The ascension of Charles II in 1660 and the beginning of the Restoration marked the "economic exit from medievalism" toward revitalization for seventeenth-century England (Minchinton 1969: 11).

Scholars generally credit this financial regeneration to three fundamen-tal shifts (Wilson 1984). First, the emphasis in trade went from internal to external markets and sources of supply. Second, new markets were created abroad through trade and colonization, resulting in demand for bulk com-modities and luxuries by Asia, Africa, and the American colonies (Nash 1999: 95; Sheridan 1973: 414). Third, once those markets were established, imports in the form of raw materials coming from the New World colonies and East Indies aided the growth of a substantial re-export trade from Eng-land's central ports, placing the Crown in an advantageous position relative to other European competitors (Frank 1978: 78).

These transformative processes of trade, colonization, and expanding markets, with all their attendant activities and participants, fed into a developing world system in the Atlantic and beyond, where the colonies served as "subeconomies" (Frank 1978: 79). By providing raw materials like tobacco, colonists relied on manufactured goods shipped from England's core ports, including London and Bristol, to colonial ports and internal riverine waterways, especially in the Chesapeake. In this scenario, peripheral areas were divided into two zones: the semiperipheral zone consisted of semiurban areas such as Boston that contained some of the attributes of the core area, and the larger periphery included colonies of scattered populations in the Caribbean and Chesapeake.

This colonial expansion, led by England and other Western European countries, was unique in that it integrated the economies of Europe and the New World. Chief among the forces driving these New World economies was the reliance on staple crops that helped contribute to the economic development of the early modern world and to an emerging capitalist world system predicated on European and Anglo-American dominance. As a desirable commodity, tobacco played a central role in these developments (Náter 1999: 254). The overall appeal of tobacco made it a target commodity that could easily be grown and harvested for profit. The same could be said for sugar. As Russell Menard (2007: 310, 323) observes, the British Empire was built on sweetness and smoke.

Between 1610 and 1640, England's foreign trade increased tenfold, making foreign investments in trade and colonization well worth the risks (Beaud 1983: 28). The uncertainties of the long-distance colonial trade instigated important institutional changes involving greater sums of investment capital moving through merchant firms, more efficient credit arrangements, and insurers whose interests were a blend of both private and state investments (Hamshere 1972; Price 1978; Wilson 1984). In addition, the demand for goods from the New World colonies forced England to find new and innovative ways of dealing with its own scarce resources. This ultimately led to experimenting with "cost-reducing technologies," such as early mechanization, that would eventually lead to industrialization (Price 1978: 123).

One of the first capital investments in foreign trade was the establishment of tobacco cultivation in the Caribbean and Chesapeake regions of the New World colonies. Tobacco met all of the conditions necessary for success: it fit

within the agrarian traditions of England's past, it was a sought-after commodity, and it literally grew like a weed, especially in the rich soils of Maryland and Virginia.

The history of the rise of British hegemony is not complete without understanding the importance of plantation agriculture. As Menard observes,
the financial gains realized by the tobacco and sugar planters were made
possible through the ability to "sell their products at lower prices, thus bring-
ing their products within the budgets of ever more consumers" (Menard
2007: 310). In this way, "the resulting market growth for plantation crops
fueled the expansion of the English Atlantic" (Menard 2007: 310). In other
words, plantation agriculture was central to the development of empire. In
this regard, the reliance on and investment in plantation monocrops such
as tobacco and sugar were the life blood of the first British Empire. Menard
(2007: 312) suggests that the passage of the Navigation Acts in the 1650s
signaled the early formation of the British Empire, further bolstered by Oliver Cromwell's Western Design in 1654. This would enable the capture of
Jamaica in 1655 and the subsequent development of Port Royal (see chapter
6). By placing control in British hands, the Navigation Acts, along with the
tobacco and sugar plantocracies, helped create the first vertical monopoly in
the rise of capitalism, which prefigured the rise of American business during
the Gilded Age.

Tobacco in New England

The importance of tobacco as a catalyst in the formation of the Early American Republic cannot be overstated. As an intoxicant, tobacco reduced social
tensions and was enjoyed throughout the British American colonies (von
Gernet 1995: 79). As Bruce Daniels (1995: xiii, 157) notes, between 1620 and
1790, New Englanders were often portrayed as lacking any sociability regarding food or drink. In fact, it was quite the opposite. In a double standard
at a time when smoking and drinking were frowned upon, weary churchgo-
ers waited out long sermons to the "soothing and edifying accompaniment
of a pipe" (Penn 1901: 82).

For those who objected to smoking in church, their mouths "were closed,
so to speak, by their own pipes" (Apperson 1916: 64). Tavern life thrived in

New England: a pint of ale and a smoke were accepted pastimes, even among ministers, unless they violated some Puritan notions of moderation. Some formal attempts to regulate smoking were made. The "clinking of flints and steel and the clouds of smoke" became such a nuisance that in 1669 a law was enacted in the Massachusetts Bay Colony that prohibited both smoking on or near church grounds and smoking on the Sabbath (Penn 1901: 82).

This law was actually preceded by the Massachusetts Court's 1634 decision to prohibit smoking by two or more persons publicly or privately as well as the Blue Laws of 1650, where the General Court of Connecticut prohibited smoking under the age of twenty-one (Dow 1988: 63; Field 1897: 23; Robert 1967: 105; Apperson 1916: 65). Other restrictions prohibited smoking in public, including "the street, hiwayes, or any barnyards, or upon training dayes, in any open places, under the penalty of six pence for each offense against this order" (Apperson 1916: 65).

What can be said in general about Puritan attitudes toward tobacco and smoking? As historian Bruce Daniels (1993: 122) observes, Puritan New Englanders "enjoyed sex, beer, and time free from work. They may have been harsh in judging sinners, but they were clear and fairminded when they applied standards, not bigoted and hypocritical." In this vein, Daniels (1993: 122–23, 127) states that Puritan attitudes toward leisure and recreation were both complex and ambiguous, as Puritan folk sought to bridge the gap between their ideals and the realities of their everyday lives. This ambiguity therefore created an overall ambivalence of "conflicting impulses" in the recognized need for relaxation, which could "refresh . . . body and soul" while maintaining godly behavior and attitudes in the form of self-denial in the community. Drunkenness, gluttony, and particularly gambling were thus highly frowned upon. Daniels does not specifically mention smoking tobacco. But he does note that much of Puritan life revolved around conversation and food, so tavern life was important (Daniels 1993: 1420143). In this context, alcohol fostered fellowship and sociability. Given that smoking often accompanied drink, smoking in taverns was most likely acceptable; however, smoking tobacco and many other activities could also be considered to be in violation of the Sabbath. Context was all important until the relaxing of such tensions of life's duality by the mid-eighteenth century.

Tobacco in the Chesapeake

Like New Englanders, Virginians were not exempt from the law; if caught missing church on Sunday, the offender paid a steep fine consisting of fifty pounds of tobacco (Hawke 1988: 23). Despite such stringent regulations, most colonists ignored them, enjoying the pleasures of a long, hot smoke. Although tobacco and smoking were common throughout the colonies, the role of tobacco figured most prominently in the political economy and social formation of Chesapeake society in Maryland and Virginia; it was here that the majority of tobacco was produced, which would have significant consequences for the region, for Britain, and eventually for a newly formed America. The predominance of tobacco in the Chesapeake could be attributed to five major factors: (1) the investment in tobacco cultivation and trade; (2) agricultural initiatives; (3) immigration and settlement; (4) a reliance on tobacco and its cultivation and processing; and (5) the adoption of enslaved labor. Each is discussed in the following sections as contributing to Chesapeake life in significant ways.

The Investment in Tobacco Cultivation and Trade

Although three geographical areas became host to tobacco as a key crop, including England, where it was briefly grown, the English Caribbean initially dominated the tobacco trade, only to be superseded by the Chesapeake colonies of North America. The amount of tobacco cultivated in the New World colonies provided an important source of revenue for both the royal treasury and the colonial governments of Virginia and Maryland. Following the world-systems model, Virginia and Maryland were viewed as the prime investment opportunities that promised quick returns, a prospect that seemed both reasonable and exciting (Kulikoff 1986: 23).

As John McCusker and Russell Menard (1991: 118) state, "the boom was on" for Virginia tobacco production and trade. Between 1617 and 1623, shiploads of almost 5,000 hopeful planters, with an initial outlay of 100,000 pounds sterling from English investors, sealed England's commitment to the Chesapeake tobacco trade. Jacob Price and Paul Clemens (1987: 37–38) observe that it was initially the small investors who were willing to take a risk on Chesapeake tobacco. But this shifted between 1685 and 1689, when high import duties and a tighter regulatory grip imposed by the Crown (James II) forced the small investors to pull out and be overtaken by wealthier stakeholders, who had the financial resources to meet the demands of large tobacco consignments in the overseas trade. Despite the initial attractiveness of high returns for investors, the Chesapeake tobacco market was plagued by a series of dramatic downturns and upswings throughout the seventeenth century and into the early eighteenth century. What saved the trade was an expanding market for tobacco, combined with population growth in the Chesapeake, which allowed planters and investors to weather temporary setbacks (McCusker and Menard 1991: 122). Once the tobacco trade was set in motion, there was no turning back: tobacco was as much a part of Chesapeake life as air and water are for everyday human survival.

Agricultural Initiatives

Although labor-intensive, tobacco required less acreage than grains, grew quickly, and could thrive in the soils and climate of the Chesapeake (Middleton 1953: 95). Tobacco farms were established in parts of Maryland and Virginia, predominantly the tidewater and piedmont areas closer to the coast, where the plants could be harvested and packed into large barrels or hogsheads, transported, and then shipped off to England. In his visit to Maryland in 1638, Englishman George Alsop captured the labor-intensive nature of tobacco farming: as the "only solid Staple Commodity of this Province," it required early spring seed sowing, followed by the transplanting of the seedlings in June. The tobacco was harvested by mid-September, and "by a convenient attendance upon time, to its perfection, it [was] then tyed up in bundles, and packt into Hogs-heads, and then laid by for the Trade" (Alsop 1638: section 60).

The Chesapeake, a geographical region that was and still is punctuated by rolling hills, coastal swamp and shore, stands of forest, abundant streams, and rivers, has had the blessings of rich soils and mild climate. Native Americans who lived in the region had a veritable garden that was carefully cultivated and harvested, such that food was often plentiful year-round. The Chesapeake region is defined by the Chesapeake Bay to the east, rivers to the north and south, and the Blue Ridge Mountains to the west (Kulikoff 1986: 18).

As the economic lifeline in the region, tobacco cultivation played a dominant role in settlement choices among planters. For example, Craig Lukezic (1990) was able to demonstrate that such decisions made by planters were conscious choices. By utilizing historical maps and data from archaeological surveys, Lukezic correlated the spatial relationships of known settlements to various environmental and social factors in seventeenth-century tidewater Virginia, including location of navigable water, roads, drinking water, soil type, and proximity to neighbors. Of all these factors, soil type and location were the most important in purchasing arable land for tobacco cultivation (Lukezic 1990: 14–16).

As the tobacco economy in Maryland and Virginia shaped colonial settlement patterns throughout the region, tobacco cultivation required some experimentation (Russo and Russo 2012: 7). The bitter-tasting and potent tobacco variety *N. rustica* was considered unappealing by the English. Interestingly, partly because of *N. rustica*'s high potency, Native American communities often mixed it with other plant products before smoking it (Brown 1989: 313). After some testing of other varieties by Jamestown colonist John Rolfe, *N. tabacum* (a South American variety known as Orinoco tobacco) became the preferred leaf for commercial production (Winter 2000a: 93). Planted in Maryland, Orinoco was coarser and stronger, with a more robust leaf, in contrast to another variety of *N. tabacum* (the milder version described as "sweet-scented," the tobacco of choice among Virginia planters) (Middleton 1953: 97). The timing of the shift from *N. rustica* to *N. tabacum* is unknown, but an exciting discovery in the archaeological excavations at Colonial Jamestown may offer some clues. In 2007 researchers reported the discovery of 400-year-old tobacco seeds from one of the first wells established in the colony. DNA testing of the three tobacco seeds could provide some of the earliest evidence of tobacco cultivation at Jamestown and shed light on Rolfe's experiments and the timing of the transition to *N. tabacum* (Historic Jamestown 2007).

With its rounder leaf and smaller fiber, this sweet-scented tobacco thrived in the rich soils of the Potomac, James, York, and Rappahannock river valleys (Middleton 1953: 97; Walsh 2010: 149). In the counties along the river shores, planters would cultivate either variety of *N. tabacum*. Unlike the tobacco-dominated areas, the lower James River and Eastern Shore concentrated on mixed farming, provisioning, and naval stores for colonial export markets (Coombs 2011: 335–37).

Although a distinction was made between the two main varieties, a number of other species were planted. To complicate matters, Chesapeake planters also realized that varying soil types yielded different results (Walsh 2010: 147). To avoid confusion for tobacco inspectors and merchants, however, other varieties were classified as Orinoco or as sweet-scented. Curiously, the sweet-scented variety actually weighed more when packed in a hogshead. But shipments were charged by hogshead rather than by weight, so this was a more economically viable option. Sweet-scented tobacco plants were more resilient, lasting up to six to eight years in the same plot (Walsh 2010: 147, 149). Because the two strains performed differently, with Orinoco being adaptable to a wider range of soils, the once parallel developments in prices for the two strains diverged after the 1670s, thus impacting the subregional economies in the Chesapeake (Walsh 1999: 62, 67). Additionally, not all areas of Maryland were suitable for tobacco cultivation, which created the need to diversify. This allowed for less income disparity in Maryland, unlike Virginia, where differences in wealth, class, and status became much more pronounced among tobacco planters (Russo and Russo 2012: 11).

Immigration and Settlement

As part of the American experience, the story of tobacco culture in the Chesapeake is fraught with great anxieties and uncertainties, disease, hardship and struggle, misunderstandings, and at times outright violence. It is also a story of wealth, power, politics, and deep social divisions.

Although scholars have debated the sequence of historical developments in the Chesapeake, most would agree that Chesapeake settlement did not conform to any dictated policy and was not uniform or coherent (Walsh 2011: 387; Pestana 2004: 14). There is general consensus that the tobacco economy tragically upended many lives, as indigenous peoples were displaced from their lands, social divisions developed along class and ethnic lines, and Africans were uprooted and sold into chattel slavery. For the English colonists, tobacco cultivation and its export became the dominant mechanism for dramatic changes and events that bridged four centuries, many of them irreversible once set in motion.

Although initial settlement was slow, the seventeenth-century Chesapeake represented opportunities for those willing to take a chance on a new venture. A darker side to this land of opportunity existed in the guise of exploitive labor practices (Russo and Russo 2012: 9). The majority of immigrants were young Englishmen who arrived as indentured servants, laboring under long periods of debt bondage, if they survived. Few women made the risky journey, resulting in imbalanced sex ratios and stunted population growth in the early period (Kulikoff 1986: 4; Horn 1994: 24, 139, 423). Colonists were also affected by diseases such as typhoid, dysentery, and malaria as well as challenges to basic everyday survival, such that mortality rates were high (Earle 1979: 100; Horn 1994: 138). The majority of indentured servants would try to secure their own servants and land once their term of servitude ended. Consequently, settlers were inclined to be independent minded, resistant to any established authority (Kulikoff 1986: 4).

Native Americans in the area initially helped the newly arriving settlers. Colonists adopted indigenous strategies for land use, including girdling, which involved removing the bark from trees to kill them quickly so that more land could be cleared. Settlers also embraced the indigenous practice of preparing dirt hills that would provide available soil for stimulating root growth in young tobacco plants (Russo and Russo 2012: 56). As April Hatfield (2004: 8–9) observes, English colonial settlement in the Chesapeake was dictated by the political and social geographies of "an existing Powhatan world," which the English often violated through poor negotiations, disregard for local traditions, and general misunderstandings of indigenous ways.

In some respects, this paralleled the experience in colonial New England. As English settlers sought dominance, they struggled to understand Indian worldviews, while regarding Native Americans with suspicion. Yet, within this state of ambivalence, colonists adopted Indian geography, utilizing Powhatan trade networks, boundaries, and interaction patterns in accordance with their own inclinations to appropriate Indian lands for growing tobacco (Hatfield 2004: 9, 37).

As in the case of New England, due to the vastly disparate perspectives of Indians and colonists, they each had their own ideas of "culturally defined rights" to land use and property ownership (Cronin 1983: 69). As they became more settled in the Chesapeake, English colonists applied a similar concept of *terra nullius* (land that did not appear to be occupied or cultivated) to justify taking indigenous lands. In addition, some colonists were oblivious to indigenous customs, which was exacerbated by repeated offenses to Native American sensibilities. In some cases, colonists were violent toward indigenous peoples, which not surprisingly resulted in retaliation, as evidenced by the massacres of 1622 and 1644 (Kulikoff 1986: 29).

Reliance on Tobacco: Cultivation and Processing

In addition to tense relations with their Indian neighbors, tobacco cultivation took such precedence over other activities that Chesapeake farmers were at the mercy of fluctuating tobacco prices and unpredictable markets (Kulikoff 1986: 23). Farm and plantation lands were devoted almost solely to tobacco cultivation, resulting in the production of enormous quantities for export. For example, tobacco exported from the Chesapeake in 1616 weighed in at just over 1,000 pounds. The total export weight increased to between 10,000 and 20,000 pounds in 1617. This trade exploded by 1630, flooding the market with a whopping 300,000 to 500,000 pounds (Beer [1908] 1959: 87; Fox 2004: 84–85; MacInnes 1926: 150; Menard 1980, 2007: 310). The Caribbean colonies of Bermuda, Barbados, St. Kitts, Nevis, Antigua, Montserrat, and Jamaica also produced tobacco (Dunn 1973: 46, 168; Fox 2004: 83). All told, England's colonies were producing a total of 1,250,900 pounds of tobacco, mostly from the Chesapeake (Pagan 1979: 253; Menard 1980, 2007: 310). Who smoked all of this tobacco? As a re-exported commodity, Chesapeake tobacco found its most important market in Holland (with Amsterdam serving as the chief node in the market chain), with Germany a close second. After 1715, however, France surpassed Germany as Britain's second most important tobacco market (Price 1964: 500–501).

During the 1620s, tobacco planters were well rewarded for their efforts as tobacco prices rose, thereby encouraging greater productivity (Kulikoff 1986: 31). In terms of cost to the consumer, tobacco prices varied during the seventeenth century. In 1604, to deter smoking and raise revenues, James I increased the import duty on tobacco from two pence a pound to six shillings per pound. For tobacco imported from Virginia, the Crown levied a tax of 10 pence for every pound (Beer 1948: 24). Combined with the prohibition of imported Spanish tobacco, this new policy caused the price of tobacco to skyrocket, glutting the market by the 1630s, when prices again dropped. From mid-century on, prices mostly remained stable, punctuated by intermittent fluctuations (Menard 1976: 402). The glut of tobacco on the market, combined with lower prices, made it affordable for most smokers and may partly explain why smoking became so widespread.

Given these conditions, scholars have debated over whether the region suffered from a thirty-year depression during the latter part of the seventeenth century (Coclanis 2011: 398). In any case the high tobacco prices in the early 1620s declined by the mid-1620s, and it was downhill from there. Tobacco prices dropped, punctuated only by sporadic fluctuations from the 1660s to the 1680s (Menard 1976: 402, 2007: 317). For example, Chesapeake tobacco prices dropped from 40 pence per pound to 5 pence per pound in the 1630s, to about 2.5 pence per pound in the 1650s, to well under a penny a pound in the 1690s (Menard 1976: 404–8, 2007: 317).

Still, Chesapeake farmers persevered in their efforts to increase crop yields. This strategy of overproduction ultimately resulted in further declining prices and compounded mercantile woes. Yet planters can be credited for improved efficiency in agricultural production and marketing (Menard 2007: 317–19; Martin 1785). The archaeological record reflects the increasing affordability of tobacco through the presence of thousands of clay pipes that have been recovered for this period (see chapter 4). Documentation in the form of advertisements for Chesapeake tobacco also testifies to the culture of tobacco and smoking in everyday life (figure 3).

Although tobacco from the colonies provided an important source of revenue for both the royal treasury and colonial governments of Virginia and Maryland, both James I and Charles I were concerned over colonial reliance on this single staple. In 1627 Charles lamented that Virginia was "wholly built upon smoke, tobacco being the only means it hath produced" (Beer [1908] 1959: 91). Despite the ups and downs of the market, tobacco still proved lucrative. According to the London Port Books, in 1686 tobacco accounted for 68 percent of the total value of all raw materials imported from North America, making it the most important crop of the seventeenth century (Fox 2004: 85; Zahedieh 1994: 243, 247, 257).

During the growing season, daily life in the Chesapeake revolved around tobacco. Cultivation and harvesting required attention, including land clear-

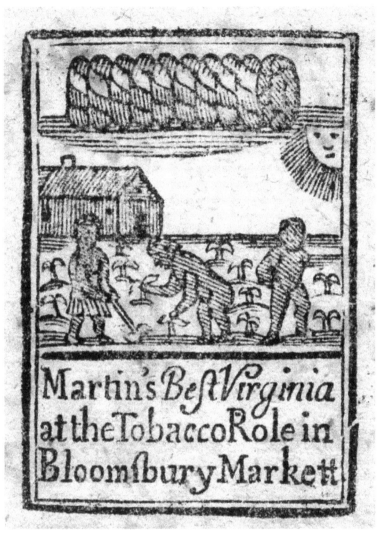

Figure 3. An eighteenth-century advertisement for Chesapeake tobacco, "Martin's Best Virginia at the Tobacco Role in Bloomsbury Market." Courtesy of the British Museum, London.

ing, transplanting tiny seedlings, weed maintenance, pruning, harvesting, stalking, drying, and curing (Breen 1985: 51; Davis 1962: 287–88; Robert 1967: 63; Russo and Russo 2012: 55). Once the tobacco was harvested, it was tightly packed into large barrels or hogsheads, sometimes causing them to burst. The large barrels, weighing between 400 and 800 pounds, were then shipped back to England, where the tobacco leaves were processed for re-export (Breen 1985: 51).

The necessity of having to ship tobacco back to England for processing was predicated on a few key factors. First, Britain needed raw materials to create manufactured goods for the colonial trade. Second, with the goal of achieving more control and self-sufficiency, Britain considered reducing its dependency on trade with European neighbors. In addition, the enactment of the seventeenth-century English Navigation Laws—which were not modified until 1786—"gave English merchants and shipowners an almost complete monopoly of trade with the colonies" (Davis 1962: 296). Under a different set of circumstances, direct shipments to trade partners would effectively have cut England off as the middleman, but the stifling laws prevented this from happening (Davis 1962: 296). Finally, the export of raw materials back to England stimulated domestic manufacturing, thereby creating jobs. Any surplus goods resulting from British manufacturing could then be re-exported to other countries, further adding to England's coffers (McCusker and Menard 1991: 38; Davis 1962: 286–96).

Although imported goods such as ceramics have been studied extensively, the material culture of tobacco cultivation has received minimal attention. By examining this body of artifacts, we can glean valuable information about agricultural innovation, culture change, and regional economic development (King 1997: 208; Ranzetta 2005: 82). The material culture of tobacco farming involves an array of implements and structures, including hogsheads (barrels), hoes, tobacco presses, barns, and flues used in curing tobacco, which is a crucial step in tobacco production. According to archaeologist Julia King (1997: 214), air curing (which involved hanging tobacco from louvers in barns) was the only method used in Chesapeake tobacco farming until the early nineteenth century. Taking an archaeological perspective, King (1997) investigated the transition from air curing to open fires and tobacco flues, processes that imparted a smoky flavor to the tobacco.

Flue-curing by supplying heat from a fire box or furnace that involved a series of adjustable pipes stepped up the drying process by introducing higher temperatures and drier air (King 1997: 215, 225). In her research King utilized historical documents and investigated flue equipment and barns throughout southern Maryland. Based on her findings, King (1997: 231–35) was able to link actual farmers to specific barns on the landscape. Unfortunately, experimentation with flue curing did not rescue Maryland's sagging tobacco economy. But King gained further insight into the growers' motivations by researching the material manifestation of these innovative attempts.

Kirk Ranzetta (2005) took this one step further by researching nineteenth-century tobacco barns in St. Mary's County, Maryland. Partly inspired by King's research and a previous field study of tobacco barns in Calvert County, Maryland, he referred to the barns as "primary sources" in an effort to determine the cultural, economic, and technological shifts that played a role in Maryland's nineteenth-century tobacco farming. The barns, as material culture, provided "a rich narrative about the farmers, slaves, carpenters, and families who built them" (Ranzetta 2005: 93).

The Adoption of Enslaved Labor

As archaeologist James Deetz (1993: 9) explains, two major forces shaped the lives of Virginia colonists: tobacco and "the labor to produce it." The labor was provided by the importation of enslaved Africans, who were brought to Virginia early on. The first recorded purchase of African slaves in Virginia was in 1619 by George Yeardley at the Flowerdew Hundred Plantation (Deetz 1993: 10; Kiser 2013). Thus began a sad chapter in American history and tobacco's direct link to the African slave trade.

To understand how Virginia planters came to rely on African slave labor, it is important to consider the prevailing views in Chesapeake historiography. Chief among these is Russell Menard's (1977) thesis that a labor shortage in indentured servants (mainly young white men) in the 1660s and 1670s spurred Virginia planters to transition to an alternative labor supply. The labor crisis was attributed to a number of factors, including a rising demand for household labor and the availability of cheap land, which increased acreage for tobacco planting when planters lacked the labor to work it. This labor crisis resulted in the necessity to seek slave labor from Africa, not because the planters preferred African slave labor but because they had few choices.

As Menard argues, this labor crisis predated the widespread adoption of slave labor; this ultimately led to a rise in servant prices, not a greater use or preference for slaves. As the shortage continued, however, a slave-based economy was deemed necessary and was therefore established between the late seventeenth and early eighteenth centuries in the midst of an economic downturn and declining tobacco prices. Menard's argument makes sense in view of certain realities that the planters faced. One factor was expense, as slaves were more costly than indentured servants. Another concern was that high mortality rates made slaves a risky venture (Clemens 2011: 394). Why resort to the costs of the African slave market when servants could be worked just as hard and be more easily controlled?

John C. Coombs (2011) questions the validity of Menard's argument. In his article "The Phases of Conversion," he argues that the transition from indentured servitude to slave labor in the Chesapeake derived from the deliberate choice to adopt slave labor, which was facilitated by the wealthiest and most well-connected planters. In fact, the need for labor was ongoing. Coombs stresses that the planters had committed to African slave labor by the mid-seventeenth century and that the transition to slave labor was gradual and consistent, not provoked by the labor crisis of the 1660s and 1670s. As Paul Clemens (2011: 395) suggests, the true motives of the Virginia planters in choosing slave labor may never be known, but their reasoning may partially be explained by a sense of greater control of the labor supply and the management of coerced labor. Although Coombs does not resolve this question, he does present nuances in timing and intention.

In carefully examining the timing of the importation of African slaves to the English colonies in the 1670s and 1680s, Douglas M. Bradburn and John C. Coombs (2006: 151) advocate for a reconsideration of declining tobacco prices. Instead, they propose that Virginia turned to slavery during a time of economic diversification and expansion, when enslaved labor became increasingly available through the West Indian slave trade. The diversity that they propose can be seen in changing demographics and population growth, the regional shipbuilding industry, trade with Native Americans, acquisition of new lands, local and other colonial exchange networks, trade with the West Indies, increased craft specialization, and, most importantly, the integration of the Chesapeake into the Atlantic economy, where the slave trade was already well established (Bradburn and Coombs 2006: 145, 151).

Bradburn and Coombs (2006: 142) suggest that the adoption of slavery was a gradual transition that occurred in four phases. In this four-phase process, investments in slaves were based on location, economic need, and wealth (Coombs 2011: 360). The first phase, in the first half of the seventeenth century, was characterized by the embryonic stages of England's involvement in the slave trade, when well-connected planters had greater access to enslaved Africans, albeit in small numbers. The second phase, in the 1650s to 1670, witnessed the advent of an intercolonial slave trade and "limited direct deliveries from Africa, [which] facilitated the expansion of slave ownership throughout the ranks of the county-level gentry" (Coombs 2011: 360). The third phase, which lasted from 1670 to the 1690s, was characterized by a sizable slave labor force, which now included middling planters. By the fourth and final phase ordinary planters were investing in enslaved Africans (Coombs 2011: 360). Slavery had become entrenched in the Chesapeake by the eighteenth century.

Ultimately, the cultivation and trade of tobacco contributed to development of the institution of slavery in America. Slave labor made the whole endeavor possible and by doing so changed the course of the American experience forever. Although the causal relationships between the Chesapeake tobacco trade and slavery may not be fully agreed upon by scholars, the transition to and eventual dependency on enslaved labor would become a tragic reality. By the mid-1700s slavery was well entrenched in the Chesapeake, establishing an institution that resulted in a long and bloody Civil War a century and a half later and would create deep divisions in the American psyche that still resonate today.

Outcomes and Social Realities of the Colonial Chesapeake

Like much of America, Chesapeake society formed out of the immigrant experience (whether white or black, free, indentured, or enslaved) and therefore cannot be fully understood without accounting for its relation to tobacco and the tobacco economy. As James Horn (1994: 142) astutely observes, tobacco permeated every aspect of Chesapeake life, impacting the "character and pace of immigration, population growth, settlement patterns, husbandry, land use, transatlantic trade, the development of the home market, manufacture, opportunity, standards of living, and government policy."

The creation of a society of English immigrants, Native Americans, and Africans produced a unique set of social and political dynamics in the formation of the Early Republic. Tobacco and smoking played critical roles in the narrative of forging American identities in this early modern period. As tobacco plantations redefined the Chesapeake landscape, English immigrants came in waves, seeking opportunity in a new and unfamiliar place. The surge of immigrants, which peaked between 1639 and 1660, provided the cheap labor needed to work the tobacco plantations (Horn 1994: 25).

English immigrants included free whites, indentured servants, merchants, and some disaffected sons of the gentry seeking a new start, drawing from all walks of life (Horn 1994: 423). Upon reaching the tobacco coast, however, the immigrants met their Indian neighbors but made "little effort to create a biracial society" on an equal footing (Horn 1994: 132). Ethnocentric convictions of cultural superiority and the "otherness" of alien peoples, combined with expansionist interests, precluded any true compromise or consensus and helped justify the adoption of slavery. Overall, Anglo attitudes toward Indians and blacks were shaped by a general "ragtag of racial and cultural prejudice" (Horn 1994: 149). Colonists in Maryland tried to avoid some of the tragic mistakes that Virginia colonists had made with the Powhatan Indians. Instead of appropriating Indian lands, the colonists in Maryland acquired land through purchase and treaties (Russo and Russo 2012: 11).

By the eighteenth century, however, Chesapeake society had lost any semblance of social fluidity, resulting in more clearly articulated social boundaries. The wealthier planters and merchants served as political officeholders and leaders, with greater access to privileges, although the wealthier gentry was not a homogenous group, as Coombs (2011: 336) points out. In this hierarchical arrangement, the middling and lower classes remained subordinate, although moderate opportunities for upward mobility did exist.

As communities became well established and social distinctions were formalized, Virginia planters began to view themselves as the new elite, on a par with the British landed gentry they emulated (Shackel and Little 1994: 9). Educated and engaged in the philosophical and scientific ideas of the Enlightenment, the new elite "participated fully in the new world of metropolitan consumer goods, adopting the genteel manners and refined ways of life that the acquisition of fashionable clothing, dining wares, and household furnishings facilitated" (Walsh 2010: 627). The economic and social framework of the Chesapeake was well established by the eighteenth century and would remain so until the 1830s (Russo and Russo 2012: 162). The society that had emerged out of the convergence of regionally distinctive forces was still marked by English attitudes, social norms, and customs. But as England grew more culturally distant, life in the Chesapeake flourished as something uniquely American, driven by the human desire for tobacco and the sublime glory of smoke.

Conclusion

The tobacco-centered economy in the Chesapeake persisted for over three centuries. The American Revolution temporarily put a halt to the international export trade. But after the war Chesapeake planters revitalized their investments in tobacco to recoup their losses in revenue. They enjoyed success until 1792, when a plethora of misfortunes made tobacco a less viable option (Walsh 1999: 77). Cultivation continued in some areas, but by the mid-nineteenth century it had become increasingly difficult to justify an economy based on human bondage, a system that effectively diminished the previous achievements of the planters, as it "warped and corroded Chesapeake society" (Walsh 2010: 637).

With the shift from indentured servitude to slavery, Allan Kulikoff (1986: 319) maintains that the first Africans who came from the West Indies before 1660 adapted better than enslaved Africans who arrived a few decades later. The growing population of enslaved Africans resulted in deteriorating and often harsh living conditions on many Chesapeake plantations, especially with the enactment of the slave codes of the 1660s, which enforced bondage based on race (Russo and Russo 2012: 95).

Despite the hardships that they shared, Africans and later African Americans forged vibrant cultural communities within the bleak constraints of slave life. Multidisciplinary studies of the archaeology of quarters, plantation landscapes, and material culture reveal the vitality of these communities and provide a glimpse into how enslaved Africans negotiated their daily lives on Chesapeake plantations. This includes the study of clay tobacco pipes archaeologically recovered from quarters on Chesapeake plantation sites, discussed in chapter 4.

4

The Practice and
Material Culture of Smoking

We have a rich body of evidence for the material culture of smoking from late Elizabethan times well into the nineteenth century. Archaeological remains, shipping records and probate inventories, treatises and pamphlets, and works of art (most notably in Dutch genre and still life paintings) all provide evidence for the materiality of tobacco smoking. The greatest repository of archaeological evidence is represented by the thousands of white clay tobacco pipes found at historical sites. The ubiquitous clay pipe has survived a number of archaeological contexts and environments, yielding its secrets about past human behaviors.

The Art of Pipe Making

One of the ways in which archaeologists can determine the impact and nature of smoking is to study the manufacture of the pipes themselves. They present another window into a growing commercial industry that first developed in England in the sixteenth century, with pipe smoking dating back to the early 1570s. Researchers have speculated that the origins of white clay pipes can be traced back to early encounters between European explorers and Native Americans, whose pipes probably served as prototypes in the development of English and Dutch clay pipes.

Little is known about English pipe making until 1619, when the first known Tobacco Pipe Makers Charter of Incorporation was granted by James I to thirty Westminster pipe makers in 1619 (Ayto 2002: 13; Oswald 1975: 4). The main centers for pipe making were London, Bristol, Broseley,

Newcastle, and Hull. Primarily a family affair in England, pipe production took place in simple backyard kilns from larger urban areas to small market towns and rural villages (Ayto 2002: 14; Vince and Peacey 2006: 11).

Made from a variety of clays (the most common being white ball clay) and produced in two-part molds, the pipes were high-fired in simple updraft kilns made of brick (figure 4; Bradley 2000: 108). Knowledge about backyard kilns is largely due to the pioneering work of Dr. Allan Peacey, who has devoted special attention to the archaeology of clay pipe kilns. The most desirable clays were the white ball clays, which contained a large proportion of kaolin, silica, and muscovite, extracted from Tertiary deposits located in southern England as well as Devon, Dorset, Hampshire, and near the coast at the Isle of Wight and Purbeck (Arnold 1977: 317; Oswald 1975: 10; Vince and Peacey 2006: 16). The term "ball clay" derives from their transport in large balls weighing about fifty-six pounds (Vince and Peacey 2006: 16, 20). To increase the evenness and plasticity of the clay, it had to be beaten. Small stones and other extraneous matter had to be removed, a process called levitation (figure 5; Vince and Peacey 2006: 20). In terms of income, pipe making allowed some families to prosper. The archaeological remains of such kilns, along with clay pipe remnants, attest to this family activity, as shown in Peacey's extensive work (Peacey 1996; Vince and Peacey 2006: 19).

As a source of income, pipe making was labor-intensive but generated one of the first mass-produced items in a preindustrial economy. Clay tobacco pipes became a hallmark of the preindustrial consumer revolution (Shammas 2005: 60). Clay pipes were manufactured, used, and discarded in a relatively short time, which makes them one of the first truly disposable items in human history. The throw-away nature of clay pipes thus assured a steady livelihood for pipe makers.

Pipe production required knowledge acquired through a seven-year apprenticeship system, which assured "continuity of ideas and practices" (Vince and Peacey 2006: 20). Pipe makers also deeply guarded their industry secrets (Ayto 2002: 13). Because it was easy for anyone who had the inclination to set up a kiln and workshop, charter member pipe makers had the right to monitor their craft and maintain "quality control" by keeping a keen eye on nonguild operations performed by unskilled laborers. This was accomplished by harassing them as well as searching their shops and warehouses

Figure 4. Example of an updraft kiln used to produce clay tobacco pipes, Broseley, Shropshire, England. Courtesy of and copyright of the Ironbridge Gorge Museum Trust.

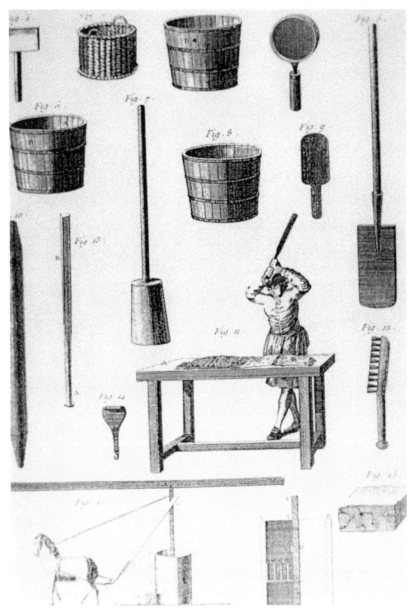

Figure 5. Preparing the clay to make tobacco pipes (from "Art de faire les pipes"). *Encyclopédie, ou dictionnaire raisonné des sciences, des arts et des métiers* by Denis Diderot and Jean le Rond d'Alembert (1751–1772).

for Dutch imported pipes that could easily flood the market (Walker 1971: 79; Clarkson 1972: 103).

Pipe makers were beset by a number of other challenges, such as securing the proper clay, having adequate supplies of fuel, and distributing their product (Ayto 2002: 13). Pipe making could be the sole source of income or could supplement farming or husbandry for single households seeking alternative sources of income (Holderness 1976: 84; Shammas 1990: 2; Thirsk 1978: 168). Although most pipe makers did not become rich, by 1650 over a thousand pipe makers were active in London alone. Other manufacturers operated in Bristol, Broseley, Colchester, York, and Gateshead, among other English towns, with the industry even spreading as far as Holland (Ayton 2002: 14; Walker 1971: 82; Oswald 1975: 9).

Bristol eventually became the primary producer for the overseas market, explaining why so many clay pipes found on mid-1600s sites in the American colonies came from Bristol. Makers' marks on the pipes reflect such Bristol pipe making families as Llewellin Evans and his relatives and apprentices. Bristol pipe makers created their own guild and charter as early as 1652, which included twenty-five members, reflecting the city's interest in pipe making as part of its economic development (Walker 1971: 84, 86). Bristol was the ideal location for these activities. During the seventeenth century, it was the leading port in the re-export trade of Mediterranean goods and East Indian spices. The city particularly benefited from the colonial trade, including the African slave trade (McGrath 1952: 196; Minchinton 1969: 33; Ramsay 1957: 144). By the end of the seventeenth century, Bristol was Britain's second largest port (McGrath 1975: 25).

Several hundred to several thousand pipes could be made at a time, such that "six workfolk will make sixty gross of pipes in a week" (Houghton [1692–1694] 1727–1728: 205), so it is no small wonder that clay tobacco pipes herald future developments in mass consumables and consumer behavior. Given that 144 clay pipes make one gross, if Houghton's account represents the average pipe-making family establishment, then one workshop alone could produce well over 8,000 pipes in a single week. Such quantities are not inconceivable. The British Port Records for Bristol in 1682 show a total of 405 gross of pipes (58,320 pipes) shipped from Bristol to Jamaica that year in addition to the 445 gross (64,080 pipes) shipped to other English Caribbean colonies such as Nevis and Barbados (Office of the Exchequer 1682). The

Bristol Port Records for 1694–1695 document a total of 3,778 gross (544,032 pipes) exported from Bristol to Jamaica alone, with an additional 4,176 gross (601,344 pipes) exported to the rest of the English Caribbean (Office of the Exchequer 1694–1695). Thus it is apparent that the production of clay tobacco pipes provided at least a decent supply to meet both domestic and colonial needs.

Whether this production fully met market demands is hard to determine. Pictorial evidence in the form of pamphlets advertising tobacco shops in England and the archaeological evidence found at sites like Port Royal, Jamaica, indicate that consumers had access to these mass-produced pipes in tobacco shops, taverns, coffeehouses, and restaurants, where they could purchase them, probably for pennies, although this could vary depending on quality. Finishing touches by pipe makers such as milling and burnishing could increase a pipe's value (Crossley 1990: 277). An English treatise of 1693 noted that ordinary pipes were sold for 18 pence per gross, whereas glazed pipes cost 3 shillings (15 pence; see decimalization conversion rates as of 1971) per gross (Houghton [1692–1694] 1727–1728: 203). The Tobacco Pipe Makers of Westminster stipulated in the 1619 charter that the best-quality pipes were to cost "twoe at least for a penny" (Walker 1977: 418). The retail value of clay pipes could also be affected by the requirements for different export markets. For example, an entry in the Book of the Tobacco Makers for 1710 stated that Bristol pipe makers were to adhere to the different size requirements for the export trade or be fined "the sume of Twelve Pence per Gross for every gross of such pipes" (Jackson and Price 1974: 81–82). In other words, they would be fined value for value.

Given these conditions, what wages could a pipe maker expect to earn? One estimate suggests that a master pipe maker could earn two shillings per day, amounting to twelve shillings per week in a six-day work week (Walker 1977: 416–17, 442). In the *Compleat Tradesman* (1684: 326), the average journeyman (pipe maker) is reported to earn between ten and fifteen shillings a week. For the most part, pipe making was a respectable occupation that derived a moderately prosperous income and a humble social standing in British society (Walker 1977: 494; Karshner 1979: 297–98). In the majority of cases, the surviving probate inventories of pipe makers indicate that their personal assets were modest (Walker 1977: 443–44; Karshner 1979: 297–98). Although much of the export market in commercially produced clay pipes was under the control of the English and Dutch, pipe making spread through Europe, reaching France and Germany and even Scandinavia, although such production never posed any real competition to the English- and Dutch-dominated markets (Goodman 1993: 65).

In terms of style, the development of clay pipes can be viewed as having gone through an evolution of types and styles over time. From 1590 until 1900 both pipe bowl shapes and sizes evolved fairly quickly into recognizably distinctive forms. Bowl shape and size generally developed together, and both changed in response to changing prices in tobacco. After the 1620s, when tobacco prices fell, clay pipe bowls became larger and more linear and stems became longer, ranging between eleven and twelve inches by the third quarter of the century (Noël Hume 1969: 296). The earliest pipes from the late sixteenth and early seventeenth centuries were therefore small and short-stemmed, with bulbous-shaped bowls that held very little tobacco at a time when tobacco prices were high.

From 1650 until about 1730, noticeable changes in both bowl size and shape took place as tobacco prices fell (Alvey et al. 1979: 249). The idea that pipe forms changed with time was first proposed by the antiquarian Thomas Crofton Croker (1835: 30). William S. Fowler and James C. Harrington noticed such changes with the pipe remains recovered at Colonial Williamsburg (Fowler 1955: 15; Harrington 1954; Oswald 1975: 29). It is Harrington (1954), however, who can be credited with correlating the decrease in tobacco prices with changes in bowl size and the development of longer stems and their relation to changes in the size of the bore hole (see chapter 6). As pipe stems grew longer, the bore hole size decreased, so that pipe smokers could avoid the unpleasant sensation of a mouthful of tobacco each time they lit up. Figure 6 illustrates the parts of a clay tobacco pipe.

As bowl shape and size evolved, the heel appeared to develop due to both aesthetic and sometimes practical considerations. According to Walker (1977: 12), the first heel appeared around 1620 as a solution for resting a pipe upright. Spurs on pipes developed sometime between 1620 and 1640 and became quite small and pointed by the late seventeenth century. Yet the addition of flat heels and spurs may only have been a matter of the personal preference of the pipe maker rather than a matter of function, as neither heels nor spurs can make the pipes rest upright without tipping over (Higgins 1981: 196). Except for the broad flat heels that typified pipes made in the Broseley style, heels generally diminished in size by the late seventeenth

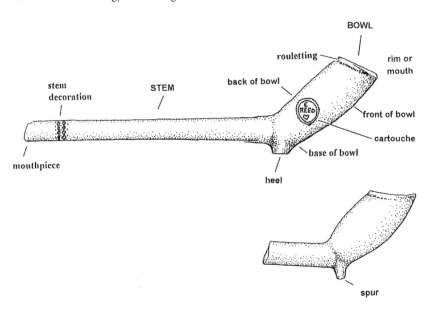

Figure 6. Illustration of a clay tobacco pipe. Drawing by the author.

century. By the mid-1700s heels and spurs began to disappear altogether (Walker 1977: 12).

As for decoration, most clay pipes started out as rather plain affairs. Most pipes were undecorated throughout the seventeenth century, with the exception of the occasional rouletting around the rim of the pipe bowl or simple diamond and dot patterns near the mouth of the stem (Fox 1999: 20–21). In some instances, however, decorative pipes have been recovered, such as those marked with the Tudor rose design, often depicted as a five-petal rose on the heel of the pipe (Bradley 2000: 111). Yet most markings for this period, especially after 1760, consist of a maker's mark in the form of the pipe maker's initials on the side or the bottom of the bowl (Fox 1999: 23). A common maker's mark found on New World sites is the "LE" of Bristol pipe maker Llewellin Evans and his sons and nephews (a family enterprise that spanned several generations). Many of the English seventeenth-century pipes found on historical sites were imported from Bristol, where pipes were made for the overseas market.

By the eighteenth century, however, a well-established commercial market allowed for more experimentation with design motifs. Spurs gained popularity in the refinement of clay pipes for this period, as did the "church-warden" pipes, whose stems (some sixteen inches long) added a dramatic flourish to complement a gentleman's smoking. Willie Graham et al. (2007: 486) suggest that easily breakable pipes with longer and thinner stems signified outward signs of wealth: "No single class of portable artifacts supplies more systematic, quantifiable information on social dynamics of commodity production and consumption in the early modern Atlantic and within the Chesapeake."

Scottish pipes were especially decorative during the nineteenth century, with the greatest attention paid to the surface of the bowl and often with the name of the pipe maker or country of origin inscribed on the stem. This may in part be due to the McKinley Tariff Act of 1891, which mandated that all imported goods to the United States include the country of manufacture (Bradley 2000: 118–19). Pipes produced in the wake of this regulation were often characterized by popular motifs, sometimes serving as a form of advertising by Victorian businesses (Ayto 2002: 34). In addition to Scotland, clay pipes were also being manufactured in the United States, France, and Canada by the nineteenth century (Bradley 2000: 114).

Pipes in archaeological deposits include those with nautical themes featuring ships, anchors, and sailors as well as nature designs, as seen in the Scottish thistle, leaves, tree bark, and floral patterns. One of the more fascinating motifs from this period took the form of personages, including but not limited to people of African descent, popular public figures such as U.S. presidents, and designs expressing political affiliations or national identities popular among certain groups such as Irish Americans (see chapter 5).

Contemporary fads reflected fashionable tastes typified in pipes as the "Ninivien" Style, which imitated archaeological discoveries at Nineveh, the Mesopotamian site excavated during the 1840s and 1850s. One such pipe recovered at the Riverfront Augusta Site in Springfield, Georgia, may have held deep symbolic meaning to the free African American community in the antebellum South because of its association with the Old Testament account of Nahum's prophecy that Nineveh would be destroyed and its slaves freed (Joseph 2004: 23–24). Another pipe that reflected popular trends in nineteenth-century America was the famous "Turk's Head" pipe (figure 7), which depicted the head of a turbaned Turkish male in various permutations. This particular motif is from the highly popular opera *The Abduction*

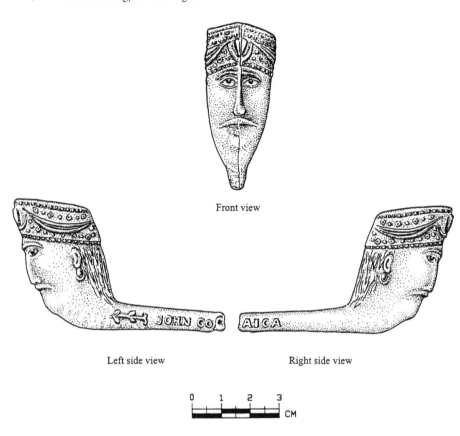

Front view

Left side view   Right side view

Figure 7. Representation of the "Turk's Head" clay pipe found during underwater excavations at Port Royal, Jamaica. Courtesy of the Port Royal Project, Department of Anthropology, Texas A&M University.

from the Seraglio by Wolfgang Amadeus Mozart, in which a Spanish nobleman, Belmonte, journeys to Turkey and braves death to rescue his beloved Constanze from captivity in a harem. All the rage, this theme of Orientalism also plays out in the paintings of Jean-Auguste-Dominique Ingres, Pierre-Auguste Renoir, Henri Matisse, and others.

Not all tobacco pipes were manufactured exports from Britain or other European countries. In fact, North America abounded in home-grown varieties, from Native American stone and calumet pipes to red clay pipes made locally. The first nonindigenous clay pipes made in North America imitated European designs and were crudely made from a variety of clays, as documented in the 1600s for the Virginia colony and New England (Bradley 2000: 118; Noël Hume 1969: 308). Pipe making was well established in the United States by the nineteenth century. But many pipes do not have makers' marks, so it is often difficult to discern their origin of manufacture. From the mid-1800s, however, the "socket-shanked" pipe, which consisted of a bowl and shank requiring a separate stem, became associated with American-made pipes (Bradley 2000: 118). Tobacco pipes recovered in archaeological contexts in North America were also made from a variety of other materials, including tin, iron, stone, porcelain, wood, and composites.

A host of factors contributed to changes in materials and smoking equipment. For example, Bradley (2000: 120–21) suggests that iron tobacco pipes, which reached their popularity in the late eighteenth century, were used during more "robust" pastimes like hunting or traveling, whereas porcelain pipes, popular in the mid-nineteenth century, were better suited to more sedentary, relaxed settings, like coffeehouses. The ever popular light and porous meerschaum (meaning "sea foam") pipes, made from carved hydrated magnesium silicate, were enthusiastically adopted by the middle classes in the mid-nineteenth century; the pipes were enhanced by various components made from leather, wood, and horn (Bradley 2000: 121). The popularity of meerschaum pipes may be an outward sign of greater middle-class affluence, used to distinguish themselves from the less affluent. One such pipe was recovered at Pipe's Old Corner Bar in Virginia City, which served a more upscale clientele. The pipe, featuring a hunting motif, was intricately sculpted and must have belonged to someone who could afford to purchase a hand-carved pipe of such elaborate detail (Dixon 2005: 117, 126).

Another stylish pipe from the 1850s is the briar pipe, which is still popular. Thought to be less fragile than clay, porcelain, or meerschaum pipes, briar pipes were created from the root outgrowth nodule (burl) of the tree heath, *Erica arborea*, a small evergreen (D. W. 1915). Although collectors and pipe smokers currently still enjoy smoking pipes, the heyday of the clay tobacco pipe was over by the beginning of the twentieth century, as cigars and cigarettes replaced them. This may explain why clay tobacco pipes are found in smaller quantities at archaeological sites for this period (Ayto 2002: 34).

Smoking Paraphernalia

At this juncture we have little archaeological evidence for smoking paraphernalia other than the white ball clay pipes, except for the occasional pipe tamper, pipe components such as ferrules or metal bands that joined the mouthpiece to the shank, separate mouthpieces, and even cigar or cigarette holders used in the 1800s (Bradley 2000: 122–25). Probate inventories mention tobacco boxes, but even the documentary evidence for smoking components and paraphernalia is rather meager. The paucity of smoking paraphernalia in the archaeological record could be attributed to the deterioration of such objects, or the clay pipe itself may have been the dominant artifact of smoking with little accompanying material culture.

Some but not all other ways of consuming tobacco are evident in the archaeological record. Costly and dainty snuff was adopted in the eighteenth century by the upper classes and associated with notions of respectability (Fisher 1939: 74–76; Goodman 1993: 81). Most snuff box collections are found in museum collections as antiques rather than archaeologically recovered. Although the ephemeral nature of cigars, cigarettes, and chewing tobacco and other practices after the 1860s leaves little to no trace in the archaeological record, chewing tobacco especially required other types of smoking accoutrements. These include spittoons, some of which have been recovered from archaeological contexts, such as three stoneware spittoons found at the Piper's Old Corner Bar in Virginia City (Dixon 2005: 117, 119–20).

Documentary and Iconographic Evidence

In addition to clay pipes and associated material culture, other lines of evidence can be fruitful in construing the more social and symbolic meanings of tobacco smoking. These include firsthand accounts of smoking, museum objects, tracts and pamphlets, and iconographic depictions of smoking and pipes in Dutch genre art.

When tobacco and smoking first came on the scene, a number of observers recorded their impressions of the newfound practice. An early and charming example is William Harrison's description of the new practice of pipe smoking in his *Great Chronologie* of 1573. The directions explain how to

Figure 8. Elizabethan-period instructions for smoking a clay tobacco pipe in Fairholt 1859.

smoke a clay pipe by "the taking-in of the smoke of the Indian herbe called 'Tobacco,' by an instrument formed like a little ladell, whereby it passeth from the mouth into the hed & stomach, is gretlie taken-up and used in England" (Brooks 1937, 1: 298). An Elizabethan illustration depicts instructions for novice smokers about to embark on their first puff (figure 8). Unlike modern-day pipe smokers, who puff on their pipes slowly and rhythmically, early pipe smokers ingested their tobacco in hurried gulps, which was known as "drinking" the tobacco (Deetz 1977: 19).

The material culture of early tobacco smoking is steeped in Elizabethan rituals and practices of the elite. A leather pouch studded with semiprecious stones at the Wallace Collection in London (figure 9) housing small clay pipes with sterling silver extenders has been attributed to Sir Walter Raleigh; whether it belonged to Raleigh or not, it is certainly the pouch of an urbane gentleman of means. In fact, class distinctions in smoking were manifest early on. The initial high cost of tobacco and the novelty of smoking appealed to the well-to-do, who showcased their skills in the smoking clubs and smoking "schools" of the late sixteenth and early seventeenth centuries (Apperson 1916: 27–28). One example may be found in London's dandies about town, who made the rounds of theaters invoking clever smoking

Figure 9. A leather tobacco pipe pouch attributed to Sir Walter Raleigh.
Courtesy of the Wallace Collection, London.

tricks accompanied by ornate pipe pouches, much like the one in the Wallace Collection. Other smoking accessories included boxes made of tortoiseshell, gold, silver, and expensive and rare woods (Apperson 1916: 29). London smoking clubs continued to be popular well into the 1830s (Mackenzie 1958: 231).

Not everyone saw the virtues of smoking tobacco. In his tract "A Counterblaste to Tobacco," James I ([1604] 1672) referred to smoking as that "custtome loathsome to the eye, hatefull to the nose, harmefull to the braine, dangerous to the lungs, and in the blacke stinking fume therof, nearest resembling the horrible Stigian smoake of the pit that is bottomlese." Yet James I ([1604] 1672) also acknowledged that "he that will refuse to take a pipe of Tobacco among his fellowes is accounted [as] no good company." Had the king lived another few decades to see the zeal with which his subjects adopted tobacco and smoking, he would have witnessed smoking as an integral part of human life. It crossed boundaries of age and sex and permeated all social classes and genders (as discussed by the early social historians Fairholt 1859, Penn 1901, and Apperson 1916).

Although this assumption seems reasonable, the actual evidence for who actually smoked is not fully available. Depictions of smokers, particularly in seventeenth-century Dutch genre art, can be encouraging when consulted judiciously. Although the archaeological record is instructive, as in mortuary contexts where pipes have been discovered with buried individuals (see Nassaney 2004), the iconographic resources can be beneficial to archaeologists examining general social attitudes on tobacco use (King 2007; Mrozowski 1993).

At a glance, it appears that smoking was predominantly a male activity. Much evidence supports this idea, particularly in Dutch art, where the context in which smoking occurred may provide some clues. The most common scenario for tobacco smoking in Dutch art is the tavern; numerous tavern scenes in Dutch paintings depict clay pipes being smoked or broken in pieces on the floor. Perhaps the best depictions of clay pipes in tavern scenes are found in the work of Dutch artist Jan Steen, himself an innkeeper, who could observe human behavior in this setting firsthand.

Pipe smoking in Dutch art is typically depicted as a popular pastime, usually in the context of a tavern or home. Smokers are seen in quiet repose, in merrymaking, or in the aftermath of a long night of drinking and carousing. Clay pipes are painted broken on tavern floors or lodged in the smoker's mouth and accompanied by a drink (Schama 1987: 193–201). Dutch still-life paintings often portray clay pipes as commonplace, everyday objects in a tableau of domestic tranquillity and material comfort, appearing among bowls of fruit, ceramic jugs, and other types of food and drink. Occasionally a woman or child is depicted smoking a clay pipe. Firsthand accounts support these scenarios, although they provide no conclusive proof as to whether or not women or children smoked. The lack of women depicted smoking in Dutch art is most likely due to the dim view that contemporary society took of such behavior (King 2007: 16).

Recorded observations provide limited evidence, as in the 1702 account of Ralph Thorsby, who witnessed his brother's sickly three-year-old boy smoking three pipes in succession at Garraway's Coffeehouse in Leeds (Apperson 1916: 92). This may be explained by a belief persisting throughout the seventeenth century that tobacco held curative properties. The most commonly cited manifestation of this is the obligatory morning smoke for boys at Eton College in England (Apperson 1916: 77; Penn 1901: 80). In Jan Steen's painting *As the Old Sing, So Pipe the Young* (ca. 1665–1670), a young boy is shown smoking a long-stemmed pipe held by a rather jovial adult, in what appears to be a merry social gathering (figure 10). Frederick William Fairholt (1859: 116–17) refers to English schoolchildren who included a full pipe of tobacco in their satchels, later to be instructed by the schoolmaster on knowing both the pleasures and importance of smoking "for a man's health."

In contrast, the paucity of images of women smoking is contradicted by the abundance of literary references, many of which are negative. One of the less condescending references details the purchase of a tobacco box, pipes, and tobacco for his "honorable Ladie" in 1641–1642 by the Marquis of Hartford (Mansfield 1963: 30). In *The Smoaking Age* (1617), Richard Braithwait notes that good manners will prompt a gentleman to ask, "Dear Lady, please you take a pipe of tobacco?" Sir Francis Throckmorton (Barnard 1948: 24, 26) presented his mother with some tobacco for her pipe, along with a new spinning wheel, in 1654.

Despite the few affirmative accounts of women smokers, however, twice as many are negative. A Swiss proclamation issued sometime in the 1670s laments that "servants, and even wives and daughters, used tobacco to a scandalous degree" (Corti 1932: 125). In the *London Spy*, Ned Ward (1927:

Figure 10. Jan Steen's *As the Old Sing, So Pipe the Young* depicts a child smoking a clay tobacco pipe, ca. 1665–1670. Oil on canvas, 134 × 163 cm (52.75″ × 64.13″). Courtesy of the Royal Picture Gallery Mauritshuis, The Hague. Purchased with support of the Rembrandt Society, 1913.

120), an English traveler to the American and Caribbean colonies, bitterly complained about the unkempt woman he witnessed "stepping from the ale-house to her lodgings, with a parcel of pipes in one hand, and a gallon pot of guzzle in the other." During his visit to New England in 1696, Ward (1933: 10) complained: "Women (like the Men) . . . are excessive smokers."

Other travelers also provide rich fodder on their encounters with the peculiarities of women smoking. While traveling by horseback in the English countryside, Celia Fiennes (1982: 204) noticed that in Cornwall "both men, women and children have all their pipes of tobacco in their mouths and soe sit round the fire smoaking, which was not delightfull to me when I went down to talke with my Landlady for information of any matter and customes amongst them." Dutch physician Cornelis Bontekoe commented on the women of northern Holland and Grouwland who "Puffed like blazes

Figure 11. After Gabriel Metsu, *A Woman Seated Smoking a Pipe*. Oil on panel, 19.8 × 16.6 cm (7.79″ × 6.53″). Courtesy of the Manchester City Galleries.

and carried flint and steel and tinder boxes about them" (Brongers 1964: 195–96), while other observers were "repelled by the spectacle of [Dutch] women blowing smoke from between tar-blackened teeth" (Schama 1987: 189). A 1621 English lawsuit in the Archdiocese of Essex further perpetuates the negative stereotype of women smokers. Two witnesses appeared in court: shopkeeper George Thresher and one of his frequent customers, Elizabeth Savage. Thresher described her as indulging her fondness for "stronge drincke and tobacco" (Apperson 1916: 208).

Artistic renderings of women smoking, though rare, do support the idea that women smoked in the early period, including a serene setting in a country tavern by Flemish artist David Teniers that shows a woman lighting a pipe and Gabriel Metsu's *A Woman Seated Smoking a Pipe* (figure 11). Less flattering is Jacob Duck's *The Pipe Drunk Woman*, which depicts a woman passed out from too much drink and smoke (figure 12). Flemish painter David Ryckaert's *The Guitar Player* (1641) features an unflattering image of a woman smoking her pipe as she peers over a guitar player. These images reinforce the notion of smoking as behavior not proper for most women,

Figure 12. Jacob Duck's *The Pipe Drunk Woman*, 1640/1650. Oil on wood, 37 × 31 cm (14.5″ × 12.2″). Photo by permission of Bayerische Staatsgemäldesammlungen—Alte Pinakothek, Munich.

but more associated with women who were considered promiscuous (King 2007: 16).

Art historian and critic Simon Schama addresses scenes of pipe smoking involving women in a brilliant work on Dutch culture that provides an in-depth study of the iconographic symbolism of pipe smoking in Dutch art. Schama (1987) observes that clay pipes acquired overtly sexual meanings in Dutch culture at an early stage. In one sense, the wonderful genre scenes of artist Jan Steen were a kind of contemporary "soft porn" that allowed Dutch concerns with drinking, sex, and moral turpitude to be played out in a strongly Calvinistic society. Schama (1987: 205) suggests that women who are depicted in smoking scenes or who are smoking themselves represent a kind of opprobrium in Dutch society.

Julia King (2007) suggests that the lack of portrayals of women smoking in Dutch art is more a case of being culture-specific. A good example is women smoking in the seventeenth-century Chesapeake. While smoking was considered inappropriate for women in Europe, their sisters in Maryland and Virginia were blithely smoking away, going about their daily business. The economy of their society was almost wholly dependent on tobacco, which was both plentiful and easy to acquire (King 2007: 18). Despite the archaeological evidence to the contrary, old notions die hard in the modern understanding of seventeenth-century colonial lifeways and stereotypes about women and domesticity, as King (2007: 18) observes. The narrative of colonial Chesapeake life in museum exhibitions fails to account for the fact that women smoked.

Scientific Evidence

What about other evidence for women smoking? To date the evidence is scant, but a DNA sample recently taken from a clay tobacco pipe stem recovered from the Boston Saloon site in Virginia City, Nevada, has revealed some tantalizing results. According to Kelly Dixon (2006: 23), tests indicate that the DNA belonged to a woman, which has interesting implications for future discussions on gender-based paradigms in studying frontier America. From a slightly different angle, a study of seventeenth- and eighteenth-century clay pipe fragments and makers' marks from lower Manhattan by Diane

Dallal (2004) suggests a feminine influence on tobacco pipe motifs produced by women manufacturers in the pipe-making industry.

Such scientific testing in clay tobacco pipe research analyses is becoming increasingly useful and instructive. When conducting clay tobacco pipe research, one frequently asked question relates to scientific proof of what was actually being smoked in the pipes. One way to address this question is through residue analysis, which in recent years has been useful to archaeologists. Residue analysis was attempted on the Port Royal pipes by palynologist Dr. John Jones at Texas A&M University's Department of Anthropology's Palynology Laboratory. The results were disappointing, as no chemical residues were present in the smoked pipes that were tested. This may be attributed to the pipes' being exposed to seawater for over 300 years, which would have diluted any chemical residues present.

Sean Rafferty (2001) discusses the application of gas chromatography–mass spectrometry to test whether nicotine could be extracted from pipe residue. The testing was done in order to recover direct evidence for tobacco usage in Eastern Woodland groups. Two pipes were tested: one tubular pipe from an adult male burial at Cresap Mound, an Adena site in West Virginia; and the other pipe recovered from the Boucher Site, Middlesex Complex cemetery in Vermont (Rafferty 2001: 286–89, 298–99). The residue from the Cresap Mound site yielded solid results, indicating the presence of a strong alkaloid like nicotine. The Boucher Site residue evidence was less robust but still indicated the presence of an alkaloid. Both residues were compared to control samples of *Nicotiana rustica*. In the final analysis Rafferty (2001: 299) felt confident that both samples indicated that some form of *Nicotiana* was being smoked. This finding has important implications. First, both sites date to earlier periods in the Eastern Woodland, which potentially pushes back the dates for known tobacco use among Native American populations to about 500 b.c. (Rafferty 2001: 288–89, 301). Second, the cultivation of tobacco during this earlier phase of increasing sedentism, horticulture, and regional trade networks could make it one of the first truly domesticated plants in North America (Rafferty 2001: 301).

Other such studies along this continuum are promising. Jelmer Eerkens et al. (2012) tested two Late Prehistoric pipes from a site in central California at the University of California, Davis, Archaeometry Laboratory, using gas chromatography–mass spectrometry. The results indicated the presence of the alkaloid nicotine, with radiocarbon dates indicating that tobacco was used by indigenous peoples in central California no later than A.D. 1415 but possibly as early as A.D. 1305 (Eerkens et al. 2012: 217).

Vaughn Bryant, Sarah Kampbell, and Jerome Hall (2012: 222) examined fossil pollen in the charred dottle residue extracted from twenty clay pipes discovered in a cesspit associated with a house owned and used by the artist Rembrandt van Rijn in Amsterdam. The analysis was carried out at the Texas A&M University Department of Anthropology's Palynology Laboratory. Unfortunately, the results proved inconclusive.

In another intriguing study conducted by J. Francis Thackeray, Nikolaas J. van der Merwe, and T. A. van der Merwe (2001), residues associated with twenty-four seventeenth-century clay pipes from William Shakespeare's residence and the area around Stratford-upon-Avon were chemically analyzed, using gas chromatography–mass spectrometry. A number of compounds were identified, including cocaine and nicotine, with eight of the pipes showing evidence of marijuana-related compounds. This suggests that hallucinogens were available in Elizabethan England. Whether Shakespeare partook is purely speculative.

Red Clay Pipes

Along with white clay pipes, red clay pipes numbering in the thousands have been found on New World sites. Often red-brown in color but with variations from light pink to deep brown, these pipes were hand- or mold-made from local area clays and were much shorter, with thicker stems (Deetz 1993: 91). Red clay pipes have been found in both the Chesapeake and New England colonies, although smaller numbers have been recovered in New England, where they appear more homogenous and lack decoration. They appear more frequently on plantation sites in the Chesapeake, whereas in New England they have been recovered in village or domestic settlements or discovered as archaeologically isolated finds along the coast (Capone and Downs 2004: 307). At both areas of colonization, however, Patricia Capone and Elinor Downs (2004: 315) found through petrographic analyses that red clay pipe production was a localized phenomenon. This raises the question

as to why red clay pipes were made in the first place. Did they fill a temporary gap during shortages of imported white clay pipes? Were they made by
particular ethnic groups who saw these pipes as expressions of personal or
group identity?

Such questions have sparked lively debate and deep disagreements among
scholars as to who made red clay pipes and why. The predominant collections of locally made red clay pipes in North America currently come from
the Chesapeake. Their origins there are articulated as nonspecific by Cameron Monroe and Seth Mallios (2004: 69), who prefer the term "Colono"
to describe what they consider to be locally made pipes, with no specific
reference to any particular ethnic group. Based on stylistic evidence and stem
bore analysis, they assert that the archaeological patterning of Colono pipes
in the seventeenth-century Chesapeake points to a centralized cottage industry. Jamestown served as a center of production and/or distribution, but
with no affiliation to any specific group; further research is needed (Monroe
and Mallios 2004: 79–80).

The appearance of decorative elements sometimes has been interpreted
to indicate potential ethnic affiliations. For example, a variety of Chesapeake
pipes display designs that are incised with geometric symbols, animals, and
other motifs and possibly reflect ethnic markers for West African peoples,
indigenous North Americans, or a creolization of English, African, and Algonquin cultural elements (Mouer 1993; Lukenbach and Kiser 2006).

The case for creolization is supported by Daniel Mouer (1993). He makes
a compelling (and at times humorous) argument for a long history of multi-
ethnic interactions in the Chesapeake that resulted in a "folk culture," which
is manifested in the material culture of locally made ceramics and clay
pipes. "Creolization is . . . a powerful process in the construction of historical American culture . . . [and] tends to reflect patterns of accommodation"
(Mouer 1993: 110). He believes that "the multiple cultural traditions that
formed the social milieu of early Virginia" can be seen in the red clay pipes,
because they communicated personal identity, were common, and were publicly displayed (Mouer 1993: 125, 129). In this respect, Mouer (1993: 128–29,
146) views the red clay pipes as "craft items" that represent early examples
of Chesapeake folk art. Pipe designs are noted for Native American motifs like deer and particularly stars, which were also shared by "English and

African pipe smokers as a culturally familiar symbol" (Mouer 1993: 146). The pipes possibly mirror the Indian-colonial trade network, where the pipes may symbolize economic interactions between the two groups.

Another case in point involves the red clay pipes, which Graham et al. (2007: 489, 491) attribute to being produced by laborers and Native Americans. This would account for the assortment of English and Algonquin designs found on the pipes. From 1640 to 1660 the red pipes appear to have quickly peaked in popularity relative to the imported white clay pipes, followed by a gradual decline after 1660. They finally disappeared altogether by 1700.

C. Jane Cox et al. (2005) presented a comprehensive study on locally made tobacco pipes for the Chesapeake region, in which they pinpointed specific production sites. After evaluating the temporal and geographic distribution of Chesapeake pipes against the backdrop of the creolization debate, they concluded that most of the locally made pipes were produced before 1670, with the larger assemblages dating about ten years earlier. Additionally, they noted a strong Native American influence on locally made pipes after 1670. Cox et al. also point out that the earlier date ranges for pipe production do not mesh with the increased importation of enslaved Africans, which occurred after 1680. This effectively negates the premise that locally made pipes were made and used by Africans, which is further challenged by the predominance of white indentured servants before 1680. In that regard, "if locally produced pipes are disappearing by the time that slavery of Africans is on the increase, then other alternatives for the production of local pipes need to be considered" (Cox et al. 2005). Mouer et al. (1999: 110; see Emerson 1999) also reject the view that the red clay pipes represent distinctive Africanized influences.

Cox et al. (2005) explain that although the "local pipe phenomenon is relatively short-lived[,] encompassing only about 70 years . . . it is a revealing topic for studying the transformation of colonial Chesapeake society. It appears that while early, valiant and concerted efforts were made to establish a local pipe industry in the Chesapeake, mass production of pipes from Europe eclipsed local efforts." This assessment noticeably contrasts with Graham et al. (2007: 490–91), who suggest that some of the red clay pipes may actually have been used by the elite, as indicated by the locally made pipes recovered from Structure 112 (possibly Governor John Harvey's dwelling at

Jamestown). For the 1640s at Rich Neck Plantation, Virginia, the spatial distributions of imported white and locally made clay pipes were almost identical, indicating that plantation owner Richard Kemp and his servants smoked the same types of pipes. For this early period, however, Cox et al. (2005) claim that wealthier sites lack Chesapeake pipe assemblages, signifying that such pipes were unnecessary when the planters could afford white clay pipes through the overseas trade market.

Bradburn and Coombs (2006: 145) offer another perspective, suggesting that small-scale industries like pipemaking could have been adopted to supplement the incomes of some tobacco planters. An example is one Richard Pimmer, who in 1659 enlisted the help of servant Silvanus Gilpin to produce locally made pipes, a venture that failed (Bradburn and Coombs 2006: 145). Another example is the Swan Cove Site in Maryland, the home of planter Emmanuel Drue. The archaeological remains of a pipe kiln and over 1,000 clay pipe fragments found near the kitchen indicate that pipe making was a cottage industry, which operated during Drue's tenure from the 1650s to 1669 (Gadsby 2002: 19, 25). Along these lines, Ann B. Markell (1994: 56) observes that locally made pipes serve as a symbol of social distinction for a number of reasons. They not only embody an economic strategy but also signify greater control over artifact forms, such that locally made goods represent independence as well as social and cultural differentiation from England.

However, Anna S. Agbe-Davies (2004: 294) cautions that further research is necessary to determine who actually made and used the pipes and why they were produced in the first place. This is especially critical in the effort to "distinguish the product of ideological nonconformity from the product of an attached" craft specialist, to differentiate between the contexts of pipe production and consumption (Agbe-Davies 2004: 275, 294). The evidence at John Lewger's plantation, with a highly divergent spatial patterning between white imported ball clay pipes and local red clay pipes, is a case in point. In this instance, locally made pipes were found in the servants' quarters, in direct contrast to the imported pipes associated with Lewger's plantation house (Graham et al. 2007: 491).

Furthermore, Graham et al. (2007: 491) observe that by the 1650s social distinctions could be made in terms of who used locally made versus imported clay pipes. As archaeological evidence from several plantations sites suggests, locally made pipes were more likely smoked by servants, the poor, and the enslaved, which can be attributed to socially segregated domestic spaces on Chesapeake plantations rather than to any kind of intentional ideological nonconformity at work. If this is the case, then the view of Mouer et al. (1999: 112–13) that the pipes represent creolized folk culture makes sense, at least for the seventeenth-century Chesapeake.

Another area of English colonization, Jamaica, has yielded thousands of red clay pipe fragments, including intact bowls and bowls with stems. On close study, Kenan Heidtke (1992: 34) concluded that the majority of the pipes were produced locally and made by hand, with a few minor exceptions. Chemical analysis of local clays was consistent with this assertion (Heidtke 1992: 96–100). Like the pipes from New England and the Chesapeake colonies, these were made to resemble imported white clay pipes, although the Jamaican pipes are quite crude and sometimes marked by human fingerprints (Heidtke 1992: 37). Documentary evidence suggests that some of the local pipes were made by Afro-Jamaicans, as a small-scale industry like pipemaking might offer one of the few means to make a living in the white-dominated society (Heidtke 1992: 90, 117). Although local pipemaking traditions in the New England, Chesapeake, and Jamaican colonies were probably not directly related, Heidtke (1992: 115) proposes that the timeframe (1640–1680) may correlate local production in all three English colonies with shortages in English-made pipes. Whether made from red or white clay, tobacco pipes and the entire trajectory of tobacco cultivation, trade, and smoking forged links between disparate groups of people and activities that engaged the New World English colonies and entwined the lives and livelihoods of Native Americans, Africans, and Europeans.

Conclusion

If we are to interpret the archaeological record by the sheer volume of clay tobacco pipe remains found throughout North America and the Caribbean, then this evidence alone can testify to the popularity of smoking tobacco as part of the American experience. To the historical archaeologist, this body of evidence reveals a fascinating story of the material manifestations of a popular habit that became well entrenched in a short time. Thus tobacco use set in motion a new array of habits, practices, and material culture in the world of all who smoked it. The development of the clay tobacco pipe, probably adopted from a Native American design, resulted in the birth of the pipe manufacturing industry in Europe and led to some production in the American colonies. Along with the use of pipes came the convenience of tobacco boxes and pouches, as smoking became a public pastime in a variety of settings, most notably in taverns and coffeehouses. Because tobacco was initially less common, it was a hobby enjoyed primarily by the elite. As tobacco production increased and the product became more plentiful, however, it was soon enjoyed on a wider scale by all sectors of society, by men and women alike and possibly even by children. Clay tobacco pipes became ingrained in daily life, as illustrated in the art of Dutch genre and still-life paintings.

The mass production of clay pipes, especially by the English, resulted not only in the ubiquity of the clay tobacco pipe but also in its distinction as the first real disposable commodity in a preindustrial world. Pipes manufactured for the colonial markets along the Eastern Seaboard and in the Caribbean can be documented through probate inventories and shipping records, which support the archaeological record in terms of quantity and locations of production. Early pipes were often plain until decorative elements began appearing in the eighteenth century. By the nineteenth century pipes were embellished with elaborate designs and motifs and at times imbued with symbolic meanings. In addition, tobacco pipes began to be made from alternative materials and in new styles, such as the higher-end meerschaum pipes and the hand-carved wood briar pipes.

5

Tobacco

The North American Experience

There's an old tale that a sailor lit his pipe and accidentally touched off a cannon explosion on a U.S. Navy frigate, blowing out the side of the ship. Though maritime legends make for great stories, one thing is certain; tobacco and smoking often figure in key events throughout American history. The story of tobacco itself is filled with lore, but no embellishments are needed when examining the role of tobacco in the American experience. In assessing the impact of tobacco on cultural developments in a young nation, historical archaeology can prove highly instructive.

Initially, tobacco and smoking were an important link in Native American-European relations. As an agricultural product in the Chesapeake, tobacco helped the colonies establish an economic footing. As the social fabric of American life formed in different times and places, the potent symbolism surrounding tobacco and smoking gained particular relevance. The study of tobacco in the American experience allows us to explore the semiotics of material culture and polyvocality in the construction of ethnic identities and in the negotiation of the complexities of asymmetrical power relationships. From Native American villages to early colonial settlements, from textile mills to western saloons, tobacco and smoking made their way into people's lives. Throughout these developments, identity formation and cultural transformation become part of one of the hallmarks of historical archaeology: the exploration of materiality in human life (Gosden and Knowles 2001; White 2009; Shennan 1989).

In their introduction to *Interpretations of Native North American Life*, Michael Nassaney and Eric Johnson (2000: 4–5) outline various characteristics of material objects pertinent to the study of culture and history. Although the archaeological study of tobacco usage in America is heavily dependent on one central artifact, the tobacco pipe, a single object cannot explain human behavior. As Nassaney and Johnson note, in working with material culture, the meanings and symbols assigned to objects are indeed subjective and arbitrary, including the meanings assigned to clay pipes in our attempts to understand human behavior from both diachronic and synchronic perspectives. This does not preclude attempts at analysis, however, while being fully aware of the potential pitfalls. Utilizing case studies from historical archaeological research, this chapter begins with indigenous societies at Contact and concludes with the archaeology of brothels. Regardless of period and ethnicity, tobacco has played a key role in shaping the social fabric of American life, with its earliest roots in Native America. It is here that our story begins.

Indigenous People, Tobacco, and Culture Contact

The minefield of accommodations and adjustments forced upon Native Americans by European settlers in North America resulted in a variety of scenarios, with the case of tobacco proving especially illustrative. Tobacco's narrative begins with indigenous America but takes an ironic twist shortly after Contact. The availability of tobacco, indigenous to the Americas, to Native Americans led to its utilization in a variety of forms, long before Europeans ever laid eyes on it.

James Springer (1981: 218) identifies four major components that constitute the "smoking complex" of native North Americans. These include the tobacco itself; *kinnikinnick* (an Algonquian term), which involves diluting tobacco with other wild plants; the pipe stem, which was often made from a variety of materials and decorated; and finally the pipe bowl, usually made of clay or stone (Springer 1981: 218; Hall 1977: 513). In most cases, the pipe bowl was made from red stone (catlinite), which was mined in the quarries of what is now known as Pipestone National Monument in southwest Minnesota (Brown 1989: 313).

The irony of the reintroduction of this complex to Native Americans through processed European tobacco as well as European-manufactured clay pipes after the European adoption of the pipe/tobacco/smoking complex (Trubowitz 2004: 145) is not lost on scholars. This leads researchers to ask: can the study of tobacco and its related material culture be instructive in understanding the social dynamics, tensions, subtleties, and complex interactions between Native Americans and Europeans? Several case studies in *Smoking and Culture: The Archaeology of Tobacco Pipes in Eastern North America* (2004), edited by Sean Rafferty and Rob Mann, address this question in provocative ways. This is demonstrated in the distinct ways in which indigenous peoples and Europeans used tobacco pipes (Nassaney 2004: 126). Pipes were often used in ritualized sacred contexts involving purification, ideology, and cosmology in Native North America or in sociopolitical relations, whereas among Europeans tobacco and smoking played a role in the social and political spheres but had little or no bearing on religious life (Rafferty 2004: 8–9).

To determine whether archaeological data could reveal Native American preferences for tobacco and pipes, Neal Trubowitz (2004) carefully examined the archaeological collections of tobacco pipe remains housed at the Peabody Museum of Archaeology and Ethnology at Harvard University. The collection spanned the period from A.D. 1500 to 1850. To complement his previous research on the Great Lakes region, Trubowitz selected pipes predominantly representing the Mid-Atlantic region and New England, from a varied assemblage that included Iroquoian pipes, calumet pipe bowls, disc and elbow pipes, and pipes made from a variety of materials, such as metal, wood, stone, and bone. The study also included American and European white clay pipes (Trubowitz 2004: 146–52). Trubowitz (2004: 154) compared archaeological site reports and the extant literature and conducted statistical analysis to determine percentages of indigenous pipes in comparison to European-style pipes. Based on this careful and painstaking analysis, Trubowitz came to several conclusions. First, in comparing the pipes, he discovered that indigenous pipe forms persisted throughout Native American material culture, despite the exposure to and in some cases the availability of European-style pipe forms. The implication is revelatory—despite the introduction of European technology and goods into Native American life, the continued use of indigenous smoking pipes reflects "the central importance and survival of sacred themes" that helped maintain "Native American personal and cultural identity"; tobacco pipes served as important markers of ethnic identity (Trubowitz 2004: 158–59). Second, European tobacco pipes appear alongside indigenous pipes in archaeological contexts, which suggests that European pipes were used in the more profane everyday world of recreational pastimes and smoking for pleasure. In contrast, Native American pipes were preferred in sacred ritualized settings (Trubowitz 2004: 158). As Trubowitz (2004: 159) observes, careful analysis of the archaeological evidence indicates Native American resilience in the face of upheaval and change. In the face of mounting pressures resulting from European Contact, indigenous North Americans made deliberate choices in utilizing European commodities that fit within with their own worldview (see Nassaney 2004; Russell 2011; Silliman and Witt 2010).

Tobacco and pipes also played an important role among the New England Narragansetts during Contact, as Michael Nassaney (2004) demonstrates in his study on gender roles. A 1980s excavation of a seventeenth-century Narragansett cemetery on Rhode Island (RI-1000) prompted interest and subsequent investigations into the role of tobacco and smoking among the Narragansetts. In the seventeenth century, Narragansett communities were deep in the throes of cultural disruption (Nassaney 2004: 129). By examining and comparing Native American and European pipes from this and other cemeteries in the region, as well as utilizing comparative studies of ethnographic and oral accounts and documentary sources, Nassaney (2004: 126) concludes that Native Americans and Europeans had sharply contrasting attitudes and practices regarding tobacco and its use. Nassaney (2004: 126, 128) contends that the introduction of Dutch and English white clay pipes into indigenous societies during Contact disrupted traditional practices of tobacco consumption in the daily lives of the Narragansetts and other groups, which strained relations and created new tensions, specifically between men and women. This is particularly the case with tobacco because of its strong association with male oversight and activities, especially in regard to spiritual matters. The male domain of mortuary ritual artifacts (such as tobacco pipes) and ritual acts retained powerful symbolic meanings and potency in the lives of the Narragansetts, but during the seventeenth century the roles shifted to accommodate women (Nassaney 2004: 129, 132).

For example, the traditionally imposed restrictions on tobacco use by women and children were lifted during periods of crisis in their appeals to the supernatural world (Nassaney 2004: 134–35). Further evidence of this can be seen in the tubercular skeletal lesions discovered among the population of this period, which included adult men and women, children, and adolescents. The lesions are most likely attributable to both wood smoke *and* tobacco inhalation, among other factors. This pathology seems to increase after European Contact, in which tobacco smoke may have played a role (Nassaney 2004: 130). In an atmosphere of uncertainty—created by the chaotic upheavals in Native American life caused by sustained contact with Europeans—the indigenous tobacco pipe and smoking served as a symbolic and powerful conduit to the spirit world, where female members of the community sought guidance through individualized rituals (Nassaney 2004: 134–35). As Nassaney (2004: 133, 135) states, through "a more democratized shamanism," the increased use of tobacco and new ritual objects like stone pestles—usually associated with women—"could help restore balance in an increasingly unintelligible world of death, animosity, and conflict."

During the excavation of the RI-1000 cemetery, a steatite/stone pipe was found in context with an adult male, thus prompting a ceremony held by the tribal representative in which offerings were made. The significance of this artifact was underscored by the tribe's special treatment of it in contrast to the other mortuary artifacts (Nassaney 2004: 132). Nassaney (2004: 136) suggests that the alternative uses of tobacco in contemporary Narragansett life can be traced back to the seventeenth century. Such distinctions between the sacred and secular realms of life can help ensure the vitality needed to sustain ethnic identity and continuity, as in the case of the stone pipe recovered from RI-1000.

The use of pipes and tobacco in the fur trade has been a subject of much interest. A study by Rob Mann (2004) considers the exchange and ritualized use of tobacco in the fur trade of the Wabash Valley of the Great Lakes region. Drawing on findings from archaeological investigations at the Cicott Trading Post site located in Warren County, Indiana, Mann (2004: 166) maintains that stone tobacco pipes discovered at the site support his assertion that the pipes were integral in nineteenth-century cross-cultural exchanges between Native American and nonindigenous traders in the expanding market for fur and European goods.

Excavations in the 1990s at the Cicott Trading Post site yielded a mixed assemblage of tobacco pipes, dominated by 274 white clay pipes and pipe fragments (87 percent), 17 stone pipes (5 percent), and 25 other clay pipes, including stone pipes or skeuomorphs, that imitate European forms (8 percent). What makes this assemblage noteworthy is the infrequency of stone pipes, particularly whole pipes. This indicates that indigenous stone pipes were less disposable than white clay pipes, thereby indicating the greater importance of these pipes in ritual life.

Mann (2004) explains that a transformation was required for the exchange to work for Native Americans. Fictive kin relations had to be established or reaffirmed through a ritual performance that involved smoking tobacco, which was considered to be sacred in that context, almost akin to praying. Mann (2004: 173, 176) states that material evidence for these "ritually charged 'moments of exchange'" is derived from the assemblage of stone pipes and their fragments. Native American groups most likely preferred them over white clay pipes in ritualized contexts, including the trade ritual. For trading "strangers" of a market economy to be converted to kin, a ritualized gift exchange was essential for people from a Native American gift economy. To keep social relations separate from the economic relations, the gifts had to be turned into goods and the trade goods turned into gifts (Mann 2004: 177). This paradox is what helped ease tensions and made the trade possible. Even in instances of known trading partners affinities had to be reestablished through the pipe-smoking ritual (Mann 2004: 173, 176). As Mann states (2004: 173) "the process of ethnogenesis is never complete, static, or free of contradiction." In the conflictive trade relations between both parties, the stone pipes and smoking tobacco represented both commodity and gift in the "charged moments of exchange," on which tenuous social relations rested (Mann 2004: 177).

Other encounters between Native Americans and Europeans also included the use of the calumet pipe. In terms of archaeological and ethnohistorical importance for the period of European Contact, the long-stemmed calumet pipe of the Eastern Woodlands and Great Plains played a significant role as part of the tobacco complex in Native American intergroup relations and in interactions with Europeans (Rafferty and Mann 2004: xiii). The term "calumet" refers to the specific context of pipe use and its form. Although calumet pipes were integral in specific ceremonies and usages, not all calumet pipes were made by Native Americans; nor were they ubiquitous in any sense. Based on archaeological evidence, it appears that the calumet pipe originated on the Great Plains after A.D. 1200. Thirty-one sites in eastern Nebraska have yielded right-angle elbow stone pipes made of catlinite (soapstone) that have bore stem holes large enough to insert a wooden stem

Figure 13. Soapstone elbow pipe with wooden stem, Plains Cree. Courtesy of the British Museum.

that would extend to the smoker's mouth (figure 13; Blakeslee 1981: 763). The earliest ethnohistorical references date to the 1634 Plains Apache ceremony (Blakeslee 1981: 762), although the pipe was also observed by French explorers in the Great Lakes region and Upper Mississippi Valley.

The pipe quickly became synonymous with the French term to "sing the calumet," but the name probably derived from the French *chalemel* or *chalumeau*, meaning reed, tube, cane, stem, or pipe (Blakeslee 1981: 759, 761; Brown 1989: 311–12; Springer 1981: 222). The Calumet Ceremony has been of great interest to scholars. The ceremony essentially revolved around ritual obligations involving the exchange of goods and political obligations, bolstered by smoking the calumet pipe (Springer 1981: 221–27). Dances and songs were performed, and the pipe was shared with visiting leaders or delegations in their honor, including Europeans (Springer 1981: 222).

Not all groups incorporated the Calumet Ceremony into their ritual lives. The Iroquois and other eastern groups had their own tobacco-centered rituals, such as the Eagle Dance, and remained unimpressed with the Calumet Ceremony (Brown 1989: 314; Springer 1981: 226, 228). The ceremony was primarily practiced by Native American communities around Lake Michigan, extending to the Eastern Plains and along the Mississippi River, but was virtually absent among the communities east of Lake Michigan and the Lower Mississippi, with the exception of the Abenakis (Springer 1981: 225–27).

Because the Calumet Ceremony figured centrally in Native American communities that practiced it, the ceremony eventually became a "ritual of encounter," when European explorers (particularly the French) came into contact with Native Americans (figure 14; Cande 2000: 40). Following William Fenton (1953: 157, 164–65), Ian Brown (1989: 311) hypothesizes that the French introduced calumet ceremonialism to the Lower Mississippi Valley in the late seventeenth century, where it was adopted by Native American communities due to its stabilizing influence during European Contact. For example, the Quapaws, Choctaws, and other southeastern groups focused on alliances built through reciprocity and kinship relations (Akers 1999; Cande 2000: 37, 40), so they perceived the Calumet Ceremony as a conduit to alliance formation with French explorers and priests. Archaeological evidence of disk- and elbow-shaped catlinite pipes recovered in the southeast

Figure 14. Albert Bobbit and Felix Darley's *Father Marquette and His Pipe of Peace* (1864), which shows the Jesuit explorer and missionary bearing a calumet pipe used in his encounters with Native Americans in the mid-seventeenth century. Wood engraving. Courtesy of The Historic New Orleans Collection— Williams Research Center.

also supports the use of calumets, although not all catlinite pipes can be interpreted as calumets (Brown 1989: 316).

Although Brown (1989: 327) notes that the calumet might have been adopted regardless of the presence of the French, he explains: "Through one of the strange twists of history . . . French explorers seem to have been in a position to spread a purely native complex of ideas. There were few good things that the French or any other European power brought to the Indians of the Lower Mississippi Valley, but the calumet ceremony might be the one important exception."

Brown (1989: 314) maintains that the Calumet Ceremony was a highly structured affair once established, requiring formal etiquette and rules for smoking, dancing, and feasting. Other activities included lengthy orations and recitations, gift exchanges, and physical contact. Any misstep in the ceremony could result in a failed venture for all. French explorers, sometimes tiring of these elaborate ceremonies, could be abrupt or skip the necessary protocols. A case in point is the French explorer René-Robert Cavelier, Sieur de La Salle, who refused to wait for the arrival of Natchez chiefs "who were to sing the calumet with him." Other French explorers and their parties sometimes declined the calumet, thus insulting their hosts (Brown 1989: 327).

Another grave faux pas included not having a calumet at hand, thus creating further tensions. Once again La Salle almost learned this lesson the hard way during a tense exchange over some corn. During an incident in October 1679, when his men had taken corn from a village, La Salle left some goods in exchange for the corn. Apparently this was not satisfactory to the villagers: "twenty of them, armed with axes, small guns, bows and clubs, advanced near the place where we stood" (Hennepin 1922: 78). The timely arrival of three of La Salle's men bearing a calumet averted a crisis. From that time on, La Salle and his officers carried calumets in their trek south along the Mississippi (Brown 1989: 315).

French explorers thus regarded the pipes as "symbolic armor" when presented immediately upon contact in the uncertainty of first encounters with indigenous peoples. Having the calumet at the ready could help assure some measure of safety and signify peaceful intentions (Brown 1989: 316; Key 2002: 158). As a product of interaction, the calumet served as a powerful symbol early in the American experience. Father Louis Hennepin (1922: 77), a French priest on La Salle's expedition, remarked that "the calumet of peace is the most sacred thing among the savages." Hennepin (1922: 78) noted the importance of the calumet, "the savages being generally persuaded that some great misfortune would befall them if they should violate the public faith of the calumet. They fill this pipe with the best tobacco they have and then present it to those with whom they have concluded any great affair and smoke out of the same after them."

The symbolic nature of the calumet was not lost on French Catholic priests like Father Hennepin and Jacques Marquette, who carried two religious symbols on his journey down the Mississippi: a cross and a calumet (Key 2002: 152). When the gift exchange of the calumet pipe between Europeans and Native Americans occurred, the participants existed in a Maussian universe, where "the objects are never completely separated from the men who exchange them" (Mauss 1954: 31). The obligation created by this exchange was serious business; immediate reciprocity was required of both parties to ensure that a fictive kin relationship, however temporary, was honored and that the intrusion by outsiders could be legitimated through ritual obligation.

In this sense, Brown argues that the Calumet Ceremony was mutually beneficial for both the French and Indians as the American continent became increasingly populated by explorers and settlers. For indigenous peoples, the ceremony brought balance during a time of devastating disease and warfare that plagued southeastern Native American communities. As Brown observes (1989: 327), for the calumet exchange to be reciprocal, both sides had to invest in the ceremony and the ritualized smoking of the pipe. The role of tobacco and smoking can therefore be considered a vital and essential component in Contact Period encounters in the American experience.

"A Glorious and Flourishing Country": Tobacco in the Seventeenth- and Eighteenth-Century Chesapeake

Early Beginnings: Colonial Jamestown

Another venture was brewing at the time of European Contact. Investors and colonists placed their hopes on a new settlement along the James River at the fledgling colony of Jamestown. Amid great expectations for success and surrounded by what seemed an abundance of untapped resources, the early colonists at Jamestown also faced a world of uncertainty. Their Native Americans neighbors regarded these intruders warily, and tensions abounded at Jamestown as settlers adjusted to an alien world that included chronic food shortages, illness, and death. Yet, as myths go, salvation materialized through a marriage to one person who may have helped improve the colony's chances for success. When tobacco planter John Rolfe married Powhatan's daughter, Matoaka (Pocahontas), he might unknowingly have sealed the colony's fate in a very specific way. Although it is doubtful that Rolfe's marriage had much to do with the colony's survival, his experimentation with sweeter tobacco varieties and his shrewd assessment of tobacco's potential led others to follow him, fostering the equivalent of a local gold rush (Price 2003: 186). To maintain the momentum, promoters of the Virginia Colony fired off letters and appeals to anyone and everyone with clout and influence. Doubters were assured of the colony's success, as noted by members of the Majesties Counseil for Virginia (1620), who described the colony as "abounding with all Gods naturall blessings."

To archaeologists working at Jamestown, the propaganda machine operating from both sides of the Atlantic became all the more apparent when they unearthed a collection of 100 white clay tobacco pipe fragments. These pipes had a special twist: the pipe fragments appear to have been personalized, providing a virtual "who's who" of early seventeenth-century colonial investors and elites (Felberbaum 2011). This included, among many others, explorer and socialite Sir Walter Raleigh; Sir Charles Howard, lord high admiral of the English fleet; Henry Wriothesley, patron of Shakespeare and an important representative of the Virginia Company; and Sir Thomas West, a major investor in the Virginia Company and Virginia's first resident governor (Kelso 2011: 11). Stamped with the names of such illustrious English politicians, explorers, social leaders, and officers of the Virginia Company, who financed the settlement of Jamestown, the discarded pipe stems were discovered in a well at the site. These home-grown kiln rejects, produced between 1608 and 1610, were made with one mission in mind: to impress the dignitaries. The goal was to present the pipes as gifts to the colony's backers on their visits.

William Kelso (2011), principal investigator of the archaeological excavations at James Fort and Colonial Jamestown, believes that the pipes were most likely produced by Robert Cotton, a resident of the early colony and perhaps the earliest pipe maker in the Chesapeake (Lukenbach and Kiser 2006: 164). Kelso (2011: 11) suggests that Cotton produced the pipes "to prove to investors that the Jamestown colonists were hard at work trying to produce things that would sell in England." Although this pipe dream never materialized, it would not take long before tobacco cultivation would ensure Virginia's place in the colonial universe. Exciting research by Kelso and his colleagues will provide another avenue to understanding life at early Jamestown.

Diet and Health

Tobacco, being the export monocrop par excellence, was readily available for any person living along the Eastern Seaboard. Archaeological and documentary evidence points to a society where tobacco use was widespread, regardless of gender, age, or ethnicity. A steady supply of tobacco along with reliably large quantities of alcohol and abundant foodstuffs promised a banquet for those inhabiting the Virginia and Maryland colonies. Although Lorena Walsh's superb study of the Chesapeake tobacco planters (2010) clearly indicates that this region's social behaviors could not be described as homogenous, a general pattern of generous alcohol and tobacco consumption appeared to be the norm. Lack of a sufficient diet certainly did not constitute a problem, as Englishman George Alsop noted on his visit to Maryland in 1638:

For so much doth this Country increase in a swelling Spring-tide of rich variety and diversities of all things, not only common provisions that supply the reaching stomach of man with a satisfactory plenty, but also extends with its liberality and free convenient benefits to each sensitive faculty, according to their several desiring Appetites. So that had Nature made it her business, on purpose to have found out a situation for the Soul of profitable Ingenuity, she could not have fitted herself better in the traverse of the whole Universe, nor in convenienter terms have told man, *Dwell here, live plentifully and be rich.* (Alsop 1638: section 16)

King (2007: 17) observes that evidence from human skeletal remains recovered from cemeteries in Virginia and Maryland offers a window into smoking behavior. Thao Phung, Julia King, and Douglas Ubelaker (2009: 62–63) examined the documentary and faunal evidence from this world of plenty as well as the skeletal remains of nineteen individuals, including two females, from a cemetery at the Patuxent Point site in Maryland. The good bone preservation offered a rare opportunity to assess individual diet and health and conduct a mortuary analysis from a seventeenth-century Chesapeake tobacco plantation (King and Ubelaker 1996: 106).

King and Ubelaker (1996: 110) observe that the findings from the Patuxent Cemetery reflect the generally harsh conditions and high mortality documented for early English colonists in a physically demanding and stressful environment, particularly for slaves and indentured servants. King and Ubelaker initially determined that low bone density might have been caused by disease associated with poor nutrition, but a more recent interpretation by Phung et al. (2009: 73) revealed that the combined trio of excessive meat, alcohol, and tobacco consumption appears to have negated the nutritional benefit of a varied diet that met most human nutritional needs (such as corn, meat, legumes, fruits, and vegetables) through the interruption of nutritional absorption. Factoring in other possibilities such as disease, illness, and age, the bone pathologies of the nineteen individuals indicate nutritional deficiencies in the forms of dental hypoplasia and generalized and focal bone loss (Phung et al. 2009: 73). The authors suggest that the cultural preference for alcohol, tobacco, and meat was a potential culprit in regard to these afflictions.

One of the most interesting examples from this study is the evidence for pipe wear on the skeletal remains of the Chesapeake colonists. Alterations on teeth can serve as indicators of cultural practices, including tobacco use. For example, long-term habitual pipe smoking can produce distinctive abrasion patterns on dentition as well as staining from smoking or chewing tobacco (Vihlene 2008: 6). Frequent and extended clenching of a pipe stem between the upper and lower incisors can cause notches that appear as smooth rounded wear patterns on a tooth's surface. The notches or facets can extend to several teeth; when the upper and lower jaws meet, they connect to form small circular holes (Henderson and Walker 2012: 796). In recent studies, such notches have come to the attention of archaeologists and osteologists in the examination of skeletal remains from Contact and historical sites in a variety of contexts (Richards, Bennett, and Webber 2012: 68).

Phung et al. (2009: 73) discovered such pipe wear notches in seven in-dividuals, including four adult males, two adult females, and one subadult, approximately thirteen years of age. They note that one adult male's wear was "so extensive that the crowns of two incisors were destroyed," such that "the pulp cavity had become exposed, generating an apical abscess," which probably caused excruciating pain. Among this population, 40 percent of the female skeletal sample and 67 percent of the males indicated dental pipe wear, with about one to three facets per mouth (King and Ubelaker 1996: 112–13; Ubelaker et al. 1996: 90).

It appears that smoking tobacco was not all that uncommon among Chesapeake colonists, regardless of gender or age (King and Ubelaker 1996: 112). King and Ubelaker cite further examples from a report by Jennifer Kel-ley and John Lawrence Angel (1981), who tabulated the number of reported dental pipe wear facets for skeletal samples in the Chesapeake. Kelley and Angel found that in the early colonial period 22 percent of the females and 33 percent of the males showed evidence for dental facets resulting from heavy clay tobacco pipe use, whereas in the later colonial period the dental wear was calculated at 20 percent for females and 39 percent for males, with less evidence for pipe wear facets after 1770. In comparison, King and Ubelaker (1996: 112) observe that the pipe wear frequencies for the seventeenth-cen-tury Patuxent Point sample are far greater than the averages reported for the Chesapeake area by Kelley and Angel (1981). Kurt Alt and Sandra Pichler (2003: 387) observe that dentition not only reflects the habits of individuals and groups but may also suggest historical developments. Michael Hender-son and Don Walker (2012: 797) note that staining and notches could in-dicate social status, especially among groups who habitually clenched a clay pipe stem between their teeth, where the mouth acted as a "third hand" dur-ing repetitive menial tasks. This would apply to slaves or, later, nineteenth-century textile factory workers in Massachusetts. Alt and Pichler (2003: 388) categorize such long-term cultural practices as "incidental cultural."

At the colonial site of Harleigh Knoll in Maryland, biological anthro-pologist Kate Spradley observed similar wear patterns in the dentition of African slaves (personal communication, May 2010). Both lines of evidence from the Patuxent Point and Harleigh Knoll sites suggest that this condi-tion was not unusual among inhabitants of the Chesapeake, regardless of age, ancestry, or gender. While pipe smoking, as seen in human tooth wear, can indicate the more idiosyncratic aspects of human individuality in the archaeological record, it may actually reflect a more common and widespread practice among the populace, especially when tobacco was so readily available (Bradley 2000: 129).

Tobacco Pipes of Enslaved Africans

For people of African descent, smoking tobacco was nothing new. Walsh (2001: 60–62) observes that Senegambian peoples of West Africa cultivated tobacco that had been introduced by the Portuguese in the 1500s from Brazil and smoked it in locally made clay pipes. A popular commodity in West Africa, tobacco and pipes became important and were a sign of elite status among Huedan women in the region around Savi, a major coastal entrepôt during the seventeenth and eighteenth centuries. Both local and imported European pipes have been recovered archaeologically in this region and were used as status markers in rural Heuda (Norman 2012: 156–58). European pipes were also used to purchase slaves in the West African trade. During the Middle Passage from Africa to the New World, enslaved Africans were sometimes given tobacco and European pipes to "placate" them while on the ship, and allotted rations of rum as a form of control on Caribbean sugar plantations (Handler 2009: 8–9; see Jankowiak and Bradburd 1996 and Smith 2005).

The transmission of tobacco and pipe smoking to the New World Chesapeake therefore is not surprising. Barbara Heath (1999: 19) states that tobacco may have been prized for its healing properties among enslaved Africans at Thomas Jefferson's Poplar Forest Plantation in Virginia, as evidenced by the presence of archaeologically recovered carbonized plant remains possibly used as folk medicine. Clay tobacco pipes have been used as "ethnic markers" to identify those who made and used them, including enslaved Africans. For example, Deetz (1993: 100–101) maintains that the geographical distribution of red clay pipes at seventeenth-century Flowerdew Hundred Plantation correlates with the earliest black presence in colonial America, thus reinforcing the notion of a direct African influence. Not all scholars agree with this assertion, particularly Cox et al. (2005).

A small number of red clay pipes were recovered at Green Spring Plantation, however, where the clay tobacco pipes were predominantly white. David Cross (1988: 96) suggests that these pipes were used by the Green Spring servants and enslaved Africans. To add to the social complexities, Barbara Heath (1999: 19, 56) reports the recovery at the Quarter Site at Jefferson's Poplar Forest Plantation of locally made pipes made from micaceous schist, which is a soft stone found in central Virginia. The assemblage, in addition to white- and green-glazed pipes, includes whole elbow-shaped stone pipes that were smoked with the insertion of a reed as well as pipe fragments that are decorated with incised crosses, parallel lines, and cross-hatching. Pipe wasters were also recovered, indicating that the pipes were made at the Quarter Site, possibly by the enslaved Africans who lived there (Heath 1999: 56). To Alison Bell (2005) this suggests a potential ethnogenesis of sorts developing in the eighteenth-century Chesapeake. Bell (2005: 457) maintains that red and other nonwhite pipes may have represented social distinctions in an interdependent society that was dividing along ethnic lines as colonists were slowly forging a cohesive identity of "whiteness" among African and Native American populations. Further research is needed to clarify these distinctions.

Other distinctions may reflect intentional consumer choices among enslaved Africans. In her article on the eighteenth-century Chesapeake, Jillian Galle (2010) applies cost signaling theory to demonstrate how slaves made consumer choices that helped cement social and economic relationships in a world of uncertainty. Although it was prohibited by the Virginia slave codes of the 1790s, enslaved peoples continued to barter, purchase, or trade items that not only assuaged the harsh conditions of slave life but also allowed for personal self-expression (Galle 2010: 23). Galle's research (2010: 24) is particularly concerned with the social and economic contexts in which slaves made consumer choices given the potential risks involved, both physical and psychological. Galle (2010: 22) thus argues that cost signaling theory provides a way to gauge contextual factors, particularly in slave life, where the asymmetrical power structure and the unpredictable conditions of plantation life leave few avenues for personal expression. The social and economic contexts range from clandestine and secretive trading ventures, rebellions, and religious revivals to marriage ceremonies, where "slaves strategically used costly, non-provisioned items to communicate effectively their abilities and achievements, attributes that made them valued social allies and mates" (Galle 2010: 25). The archaeological evidence of such consumables includes items of personal adornment like buttons as well as tablewares, including refined ceramics. Although Galle does not include clay tobacco pipes in her study, could the easily disposable, ubiquitous clay tobacco pipe qualify as an object worthy of costly signaling or signify any degree of social or personal distinction?

Archaeological excavations conducted at the mid-eighteenth-century slave quarters of several James River plantations, including Carter's Grove, Southall, and Green Spring, might reveal some possible clues. At Southall's Quarters in James City County, Virginia, 5 percent of the tobacco clay pipe remains found at the site were made from white clay, in comparison to the less predominant red clay pipes. Stevan Pullins et al. (2003: 141–43, 173) attribute this to two types of behaviors: (1) tobacco smoking was probably confined to the quarters area; and (2) proximity of the quarters to the main house could affect the nature of the assemblage. In maintaining their own visible displays of status, the planters' houses would likely contain fine imported goods, including English clay pipes, ceramics, and other objects. In this regard, white clay pipes could dominate the assemblage if the quarters were closer to the main house with all of its imported items, where enslaved Africans might have greater access to the larger economy outside the plantation system (Pullins et al. 2003: 10, 173).

Parallel findings at Carter's Grove Plantation in Virginia for roughly the same period also indicate a predominance of white clay pipes, suggesting that planter James Bray III possibly issued the pipes to his slaves, making it less practical for the slaves to make their own (Walsh 2001: 198). At the quarters at Utopia, an outlying agricultural area at Carter's Grove, however, Virginia-made tobacco pipes were recovered, dating to the late seventeenth century. The pipes reflect the cultural dynamics that arose from the simultaneous presence of Africans, Native Americans, and European indentured servants. In Walsh's observations (2001: 95), the locally made tobacco pipes "combine designs and techniques selected and adapted from all three cultural groups." Could locally made pipes signify a type of social distinction in reverse, where the non-elite intentionally distinguished themselves from the planters? Further research would be required to test this idea.

Clay tobacco pipes also conveyed other meanings for enslaved Africans. A remarkable find at the Utopia quarter is the burial of three slaves that may reflect West African burial traditions in the form of grave goods. In this particular instance, English white clay tobacco pipes were found in the burials of one woman and two men, with the pipe placed underneath the arm, akin to mortuary practices in Barbados. This may reflect West African influences in the burials of African-born and first-generation slaves, as grave goods (including clay tobacco pipes) played a role in slave burial practices (Handler and Lange 1978: 199, 201, 210; Morgan 1998: 642; Walsh 2001: 106). Because slaves valued tobacco, a clay pipe may have been regarded as a suitable offering to the ancestors or as a companion in the long journey to the afterworld or Africa (Handler and Lange 1978: 200; Handler 1983: 245; Jamieson 1995: 49).

Other burials confirm the use of clay pipes as grave goods. In Bridgetown, Barbados, a woman of African descent was found buried with a long-stemmed white clay pipe, with the bowl resting in her right hand. The grave was located in an unmarked burial ground in the Pierhead section of Bridgetown (Crain et al. 2004: 75–77). Handler and Lange (1978: 123, 135) report that seventeen individuals at Newton Plantation, Barbados, were found buried with white clay pipes. At the Patuxent Point Cemetery in Maryland, the person in Burial 18 was found cradling a white clay tobacco pipe, although the individual's ancestry was not conclusive (King 1996: 41–42). Perhaps one of the most unusual examples is the burial of an old man on Newton Plantation (Burial 72), which dates to about the late 1600s. A pipe that was nothing like any others that have been reported for the Americas was found in the grave. The clay pipe is West African, possibly from Ghana. It had a small hole to insert a detachable stem and is characterized by its buff color and an acute angle where the stem and bowl meet (Handler and Norman 2007: 7–8). The individual may have been an obeah man or folk doctor on the Barbados plantation where he was buried (Handler 1983; Handler and Norman 2007: 4).

Tobacco, Class, Gender, and Ethnic Identity in Urban America

Americans are recognized worldwide for their ingenuity, hard work, and sense of individuality. The conditions that conspired to create these identifiable characteristics, whether real or residing in the popular imagination, have been analyzed in a number of disciplines through the various mechanisms of political and social movements, popular culture, and watershed events in American history. Historical archaeology has much to contribute to this discourse by providing material and documentary evidence. As tobacco became fully entrenched in American culture, collective and individual expressions of tobacco use were recorded in urban contexts, particularly in the nineteenth century (Groover 2003, 2008; Mrozowski 2006; Mrozowski et al. 1996).

The subject of tobacco use occupies a niche in studies of class, gender, and ethnicity (see Mullins 1999; Dixon 2006; Capone and Downs 2004). For example, in analyzing nineteenth-century boardinghouse life at Boott Mills in Lowell, Massachusetts, Lauren Cook (1989) examines the formation of working-class identity through a number of expressions, including the smoking of tobacco. This can similarly be seen at the Five Points neighborhood excavations in New York, where Paul Reckner (2001) investigates political affiliations of working-class Irish Americans through the various insignia displayed on their clay tobacco pipes. Reckner's work (2004) in Paterson, New Jersey, follows similar lines. Class identity maintained through tobacco use is also demonstrated by Jarrett Rudy (2005) in his study of the subject in Victorian Montreal, Canada, which witnessed parallel developments to the United States. During the nineteenth century, clay tobacco pipes were produced for a world market that included a wide range of expressive pipe styles and motifs for consumers to choose from. These decorative pipes bore a number of slogans and symbols, some referencing Irish nationalist and political movements (Reckner 2004: 252; Walker 1977, 1983).

Tobacco and Working-Class Identity: Boott Mills

The tensions and everyday realities of class differences in American life are illustrated by the use of tobacco at Boott Mills in Lowell, Massachusetts, home to the many laborers who toiled in the textile mills. Situated at the confluence of the Merrimack and Concord Rivers in northern Massachusetts, Lowell provides a rich tapestry of the archaeology of nineteenth-century working-class life. Much has been written about this period in Lowell, particularly in the study of American urban history, but historical archaeologists have broadened our understanding of life in this mill town through careful excavation and analyses. This research shows how tobacco use and smoking can illuminate aspects of working-class behavior that distinctly differ from mannerisms of the middle and upper-middle classes. Such behavior derives more from symbolic acts of working-class identity than from any particular class conflict (Cook 1989: 215).

As an urban center, Lowell was unique in many respects. From its establishment in 1825, the first planned industrial city in North America was designed to process southern cotton and wool (Mrozowski 2006: 16–17, 66–67; Mrozowski et al. 1996: 2). By mid-century, Lowell could boast its stature as the nation's greatest industrialized complex. In this context, archaeological research has focused on the workers of the town, more specifically at the location of the former Boott Cotton Mills. Under the auspices of the National Park Service and the Center for Archaeological Studies at Boston University, archaeological survey and excavations were conducted in an asphalt-covered parking lot in 1986. The goal was to unearth the backyards of Boarding House #48 and Tenement #45 and subsequently excavate the Lawrence Company overseers' (managers') block (Mrozowski 2006: 130; Mrozowski et al. 1996: 3, 9–18). Also referred to as "backyard archaeology," the 1986 excavations revealed a rich array of faunal and botanical remains representative of dietary sources, glass bottles and ceramics, nails, window glass, beads, buttons, pins, jewelry and other personal items, and clay tobacco pipes. The study of these remains has contributed to a better understanding of boardinghouse and tenement life in a working-class town (Mrozowski 2006: 98).

By mid-century, as Lowell's demographic profile slowly began to shift from predominantly young farm girls to immigrant labor, boardinghouse life became less regulated. Elizabeth Peña and Jacqueline Denmon (2000: 82) note that such communal living arrangements often served as a surrogate family, protecting workers from the outside world. In their study of boardinghouse culture, Lauren Cook (1989: 215) and Mary Beaudry et al. (1991: 167) recognize three distinct arenas in which tobacco played a role at Boott Mills. These include the physical space in which tobacco was smoked; the perceived status of working-class smokers in relation to the surrounding social milieu; and working-class identity as symbolically conveyed to other members of that community.

Mrozowski et al. (1996: 67) observe that during a grueling six-day work week many immigrants spent part of their leisure time socializing in the backyard. Archaeological evidence in the form of bottle and clay pipe fragments indicates that part of this time was spent drinking and smoking. The backyards of Boott Mills's tenements and boardinghouses served as a chief space for enjoying a smoke; the other was the factory. The stems of clay pipes (the pipes of choice) could be shortened by snapping them, so that laborers could smoke while working (Mrozowski 2006: 130). These workers' "cutties" or short-stemmed pipes thus came to symbolize working-class culture (Cook 1989: 218; Mrozowski 2006: 130).

The perceived status of working-class smokers by other segments of society was less than positive. Notions of respectability and middle-class sensibilities, particularly in regard to women, meant that public displays of smoking were often frowned upon. This attitude marked the class divide between the irksome working-class individuals who smoked in public and those who smoked in more genteel circumstances behind closed doors (Cook 1989; Reckner and Brighton 1999: 68–69; Beaudry et al. 1991: 168).

As a symbolic gesture to fellow members of the working-class community, smoking the short cutties in public was an act of defiance. Considered passé by the middle-class, the clay pipe took on even greater significance as a sign of working-class identity (Reckner 2001: 105). Intentionally and blatantly disregarding middle-class rules and ideas of propriety, the offending smokers probably evoked some degree of satisfaction as they lit and smoked their pipes (Cook 1989: 218–20). This supports the idea that leisure or nonwork-related activities often provide the greatest opportunities for self-expression and self-definition (Cook 1989: 210). Kathy Peiss (1986: 40) notes that for working-class women precious leisure hours were something separate from their work life and therefore to be carefully guarded from any encroachments on their time. Having a leisurely smoke during off-hours, particularly in public places, spoke volumes about the smokers, the context of their behavior, their perceived status, and their regard for the world around them. The practice of smoking in public was nothing new. Harkening back to antecedents such as the English tavern, this behavior had simply transferred to public spaces in American towns and cities, extending to parks and the street, creating a working-class "style" that emerged to help maintain boundaries from the middle and upper classes (Cook 1989: 212, 219).

Tobacco and Ethnicity: Irish Americans

The Irish were one predominantly working-class segment of the urban population that found their own forms of self-expression. The world of Irish laborers, the "fighting Irish" of nineteenth-century New York, provides a good case study in identity politics as seen through tobacco and smoking. The archaeological evidence that illustrates this is observable in the clay tobacco pipes recovered from the Five Points/Courthouse site at Foley Square in Manhattan's Sixth Ward Neighborhood of New York and in the archaeological excavations at Paterson's South Ward, known as "Dublin," in New Jersey. Smoking behavior representative of Irish American identity took shape in a number of ways in working-class Irish neighborhoods, with the clay pipe serving as the instrument of choice (Cook 1989: 221). In these locales, social interactions were carried out almost exclusively in male community venues such as religious institutions, volunteer fire departments, labor organizations, and various ethnic and national organizations, in addition to neighborhood saloons (Reckner 2004: 248). The numerous affiliations, ideologies, and identities of nineteenth-century Irish Americans, like these venues, were neither homogenous nor unified. As Reckner (2004: 263) observes, the Irish American community was not one "monolithic whole."

In terms of their symbolic meanings, clay tobacco pipe motifs do not present merely a traditional and simplistic marker of "Irishness"; rather, they express a varied "range of Irish nationalist factions and ideologies," including trade unionism and as a reaction to hostile anti-immigrant sentiments in the form of nativist Irish ethnic stereotypes and anti-Catholic sentiments (Reckner 2001: 103, 2004: 252). Within the Irish community, class conflict and class struggles played out daily amid social interactions (Reckner 2004: 243). In contrast to Boott Mills, however, the Irish in the Five Points section of Manhattan appear to have made a conscious decision to mute their "Irishness" in the effort to demonstrate their patriotism in their adopted homeland (Mrozowski 2006: 148).

The mass migration of Irish immigrants to New York came in a series of waves during Ireland's Potato Famine of the 1840s. As a result, Irish (and German) immigrants dominated the city's workforce by the mid-nineteenth century. New York had earned the moniker "the most Irish city in the Union" by the 1870s. As Hasia Diner (1996: 87) notes, New York without the Irish "would be difficult to imagine." Of the 1.8 million immigrants who arrived in the 1840s and 1850s, approximately 848,000 were Irish. Many of them settled in Lower Manhattan because of the cheap rent and available jobs (Diner 1996: 91, 94). The best-known of the Lower Manhattan neighborhoods is the infamous Five Points, popularized by journalist Herbert Asbury in *The Gangs of New York* ([1928] 2008) and further publicized in the 2002 Martin Scorsese film. It sits at the margins of present-day Chinatown in the area of the federal courthouse, whose construction led to archaeological excavations in the early 1990s. Subsequent analysis was conducted by Rebecca Yamin (1997, 2001). Given the long-term site disturbances and the challenges of conducting excavations in a highly urbanized area like New York City, the excavation of this block offered a glimpse into the daily lives of the city's mid-nineteenth-century immigrants, including how they broadcast their identities, based on the material culture that they left behind (Yamin 2001: 3).

The idea that "wage-earning is not a career that men seek for its own sake" is further heightened by equating wage labor with "abject dependence," an association that underpins modern Anglo-American thought (Wilentz 1984: 9). In the case of impoverished Irish American immigrants, nothing could be closer to the truth. The large influx of available immigrant labor arrived during New York's industrial era, a time of urban expansion, when the city served as a commercial and transportation hub for the United States and required a variety of menial and craft labor (Diner 1996: 88). Men worked in the construction trades as bricklayers, carpenters, or stonecutters, on the docks as longshoremen, or in other occupations, including as printers, porters, or drivers. Unmarried women took on domestic work in hotels and private homes, while married women worked at home as seamstresses, took in boarders, or worked as street vendors or grocers (Cantwell and Wall 2001: 216–17; Diner 1996: 95).

As historian James Barrett (2012: 11) notes, ideas of "how one became American were highly contested"; but as immigrants gradually became integrated into American life, "it was less into a hostile WASP mainstream than into an emerging multiethnic working-class milieu that they themselves had pioneered." Irish immigrants were neither blank slates nor a homogenous clan. As with any immigrant group, the Diaspora Irish brought with them their entrenched worldviews, traditions, beliefs, values, and expectations in terms of appropriate responses and behaviors, some of which would serve them well as they adjusted to life in America (Brighton 2009: 9).

For many Irish, poverty arising from the instabilities of economic life as a result of cyclic booms and busts, low wages, limited occupational mobility, the continual infusion of newly arriving immigrants, and discrimination laid the foundation for activism in New York's labor movement and urban politics (Diner 1996: 98; Dolan 2008: 87, 97; McKivigan and Robertson 1996: 303). In fact, the social values of community that the Irish carried with them across the Atlantic were manifest in the strong attachments to their neighborhoods and parish life. From this foundation, the Irish developed a highly organized cultural, social, and political life that played out in the streets, workplaces, saloons, and union locals of Boston, New York, Chicago, and elsewhere (Barrett 2012: 11, 39; Brighton 2009: 9–10; Dolan 2008: 85, 95). In this context, the American labor movement and labor reform are largely inspired by working-class Irish social movements, such as the Knights of Labor and the American version of the Land League. The emerging Irish nationalism of the nineteenth century can be viewed as a product of Irish working-class laborers and industrial workers, where ethnicity acted more as "a reinforcement to class solidarity than a distraction from class antagonisms" (Wilentz 1984: 5; Barrett 2012: 111; McKivigan and Robertson 1996: 304). In other words, the Irish were becoming "more Irish" in the larger context of identity formation.

The material culture of clay tobacco pipes reinforces this notion. Among the many artifacts recovered from the backyard privies of the Five Points Irish and German tenements were a fair share of pipes. The presence of clay tobacco pipes is revealing in and of itself; at a time when middle- and upper-class smokers preferred pipes made of meerschaum and wood, Irish and German immigrants were still using pipes made of clay (Yamin 1997: 52). At an Irish household on Pearl Street, a handful of clay pipes recovered from a backyard privy revealed patriotic motifs (Yamin 1997: 52).

Analyzing decorative pipes from the Five Points excavations, archaeologist Paul Reckner sees symbolic connections between political allegiances and Irish identity and ethnicity. In the recovery of clay tobacco pipe fragments from the Five Points/Courthouse site, Reckner (2001: 105) examined the "federal eagle" and the circular "thirteen stars" motifs, which defined the

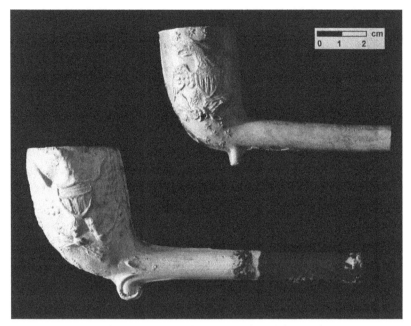

Figure 15. Nineteenth-century clay tobacco pipes found during the excavation of the Five Points neighborhood. The pipes bear the "federal eagle" and "thirteen stars" motifs, popular among some Irish Americans. Courtesy of Paul Reckner.

post-1840s patriotic ideals of trade unions (figure 15; Reckner 2001: 105). The federal eagle is a take on the bald eagle, and the "thirteen stars" alludes to the American flag; taken together, these were *the* symbols of national identity. Does this mean that the working-class Irish who used these pipes were patriotic? Reckner (2001: 109) suggests that these symbols could be construed in a number of ways because of their multiple meanings. One interpretation focuses on the tensions that existed between rival political groups in the Irish working-class community. The more powerful interest groups felt that allying themselves with symbols of national identity was prudent in terms of their own political interests. In contrast, smaller, more local groups who identified with issues closer to home, such as members of New York's tailors' unions, struggled to build their own power base. In co-opting motifs like the federal eagle and thirteen stars and linking their interests to broader concerns, they could expand and consolidate their political influence (Reckner 2001: 109). The public display of such national motifs would therefore reinforce awareness of the smoker's political leanings in the community.

Tobacco pipes from the Five Points and another Irish neighborhood in Paterson, New Jersey, reveal the logo "HOME RULE," sometimes accompanied by a shamrock and harp (Reckner 2001: 111). This embodies the long-term Irish nationalist Home Rule Movement, especially during the late nineteenth century (Reckner 2001: 111). Reckner (2004: 256–57, 261) argues that such emblems reflect the "emergence of a distinctly Irish American ethnic identity" born out of working-class consciousness, aided by such radical Irish newspapers as the *Paterson Labor Standard*, which provided an influential forum for labor activists. In a similar vein, a clay pipe at Boott Mills that bears the emblem "Wolf 98 Tone," referring to the Irish nationalist martyr Wolf Tone (who was executed in 1798), probably expresses a "conscious ethnic identity" (Cook 1989: 227; Mrozowski 2006: 130).

Interestingly, the excavations of "Dublin" in Paterson yielded a pipe that signified the Irish Protestant "Red Hand of Ulster" motif, which could be construed as anti-Catholic. The find of a single clay pipe that bears both Irish and U.S. nationalist motifs in the form of a flag and harp, however, points to "a new symbolic construction of Irish American identity," serving the need to express patriotism while maintaining pride in Irish identity. This dual approach belies the more complex and transformative aspects of identity formation in urban America (Reckner 2004: 264). The semiotics of these embellished pipes exemplify "the ongoing reworking of symbolic meanings and social identities through daily practice and struggle" (Reckner 2004: 265). As the Irish adjusted to life in America, they incorporated and adapted new modes of consumption in the reformation of identity, as the clay pipes demonstrate. Reckner (2004: 262) observes that Irish Americans were becoming more Irish than their ancestors through their various class struggles and confrontations with the deplorable working conditions of the textile mills and factories of industrialized America and therefore "more like themselves" in the truest sense.

Sex and the City: Tobacco and Women Smokers in Late Victorian America

Smoking and tobacco are instrumental not only in the shaping of class formation and ethnicity but also in terms of gender in American life, particularly for women in the late Victorian era. The social setting and manner in which a woman consumed tobacco reflected her class and ethnicity as well as prevailing perceptions of behaviors of female smokers. The act of smoking, imbued with symbolic meanings, could also reflect the changing nature and complexities of women's roles in North America (Rotman 2009; see also Goodwin 1999).

Historian Jarrett Rudy's research on tobacco consumption in urban Montreal (2005) in many ways parallels similar developments in urban America, particularly in the Northeast. His premise is that the idea of the liberal individual represented "a complex and contested process in which people internalized notions of inclusion, exclusion, and hierarchy that shaped how they saw themselves and others" (Rudy 2005: 171). This resonated within the United States up to the First World War. Even in the twenty-first century, smoking still provides one measure of legitimization among some young adults and certain subcultures, even as tobacco has been deemed bad for human health.

Archaeologist Lauren Cook (1997: 26) calls for an interpretive approach to decipher meanings of behaviors in the study of gender: in this case, women who smoked, particularly during the Late Victorian age. This period could be viewed as a time when some women began to cast aside the restraints of Victorian morality. Women were a heterogeneous group. In their individual reactions, they empowered themselves in performing small acts of defiance, including smoking (Cook 1997: 24, 34). In the urban American Northeast, as well as in Montreal, certain attitudes prevailed regarding women smokers. For example, within the constructs of individualism and liberalism, Rudy (2005: 171) maintains that gender played a critical role in determining who smoked and what constituted a "respectable" smoker. In this cultural milieu, tobacco and smoking were in the domain of the masculine world, exemplified by composure and rationality. From a man's position, women were considered biologically inferior and incapable of good sense or self-control. Male smokers "set the tone and boundaries of the male public sphere," from which women were excluded (Rudy 2005: 171).

As an activity largely relegated to and regulated by men, smoking tobacco in the socially constructed permissible spaces of the saloon, railroad car, or club was viewed as a masculine ritual (Cook 1997: 31). Rudy (2005: 6) notes that just before the First World War, even as women were "culturally outlawed" from smoking, they demanded the right to smoke. When the war

ended, their demands gave way to greater acceptance, as women gained suf-
frage and employment, growing increasingly visible in public places. During
the late Victorian era, however, middle- and upper-class notions of respectability and etiquette did not include smoking in public, especially by women.
Such behavior could compromise a woman's dignity. In the archaeological
excavations of a nineteenth-century brothel in St. Paul, Minnesota, K.
Anne Ketz et al. (2005: 86) were surprised by the dearth of clay tobacco
pipe fragments in the yard assemblage. This could be explained by the rigid
class behaviors expected from women, even among prostitutes, especially if
they wished to attract a superior clientele. This did not always deter women
from smoking, mostly behind closed doors, with cigarettes as the method of
choice. Ketz et al. acknowledge that the near-absence of clay pipe remains
could be explained by the use of cigarettes or cigars, which would leave no
trace in the archaeological record.

Sensibilities about smoking were not solely confined to middle- and
upper-middle class women. Working-class women bore the brunt of dis-
dain from their "superiors" but not from their own peers (Ketz et al. 2005:
86). Social distinctions could be further reinforced by the quality of tobacco
that a person smoked, regardless of gender. When a working-class person
smoked low-quality tobacco, this could reflect on his or her station in life as
well as suggesting a lack of taste and character (Rudy 2005: 6). Standards of
personal behavior and etiquette were "part of a larger narrative of progress
of so-called civilization," which designated many ethnic groups as inferior
(Rudy 2005: 16).

The politics of taste and the narrative of civilized behavior were echoes of
the past. Such attitudes were well established in seventeenth-century England (Withington 2011: 633). The way the "folk" behaved in terms of social
decorum (or lack thereof) did not meet the approval of the social elites, who
reinforced their attitudes through campaigns to reform and civilize their in-
feriors, much like the later temperance and improvement campaigns of the
Victorian era.

Late Victorian imagery and the archaeological excavations at Boott Mills
can provide insight into the immigrant response to the attitudes of elite superiority during this time. In stark contrast to their middle- and upper-class
counterparts, immigrant Irish women openly smoked clay pipes (the preferred choice among the working class) in public. The "taint" of public smok-

ing promoted the idea of promiscuity and belief that lower-class women were morally corrupt, as smoking reflected a woman's lack of control over her sensuality and sexuality. In the social construction of the inclusion and exclusion dichotomy, however, the behavior of working-class Irish women (as well as working-class Irish men) who smoked in public could also be construed as a subtle form of resistance through this nonverbal communication of group identity in reaction to middle- and upper-class sensibilities (Cook 1989: 211). Ironically, smoking in public became the norm by the mid-twentieth century; the act "had become hegemonic, illustrating the ability of working-class culture to negotiate at least some of its practices into cultural dominance" (Cook 1989: 220).

Archaeology cannot determine precisely the extent to which women smoked during this period, but the archaeological assemblage in my own research at the Betty's Hope plantation on the Caribbean island of Antigua offers some clues. Although I cannot definitively conclude that women, whether of British or African descent, smoked at the plantation, one excavation unit yielded some exciting artifacts among the items of "women's work," which included sewing and child-rearing. Found in association with needles, pins, thimbles, buttons, hooks, and small children's toys were remnants of clay tobacco pipes dating to the Victorian period. This could be construed in a number of ways. It could imply that men might have been present during these activities or that the strict mores of Victorian "womanhood" could be slightly more relaxed in the Caribbean context, where women could smoke unhampered. The latter view is more appealing and certainly not without precedents. In the Victorian mind-set, the family was an idealized social institution. But as in the case of their relationship with the queen, the British colonies were embraced but also distant, much like their subjects (Renk 1999: 8).

In her assessment of middle-class women in British colonial settings, Susan Lawrence (2003: 22, 28–29) proposes that no real homogeneity existed among colonial cultural practices. The American experience was quite different than, say, the experience of New Zealand or Australia. But the underlying notion of "respectability" did exist in the Anglo-American world. Victorian domesticity certainly existed at Betty's Hope with its proper comportment and refined behavior, but the degree to which it dictated daily life remains unknown. It is a distinct possibility that women smoked in the privacy of their own homes in the Caribbean.

In sum, what can we learn from women smokers? Based on the accumulation of evidence from almost four centuries of archaeological, documentary, and iconographic evidence, women have smoked since the introduction of tobacco. Contexts were dependent upon the various social pressures exerted on women's public and private behaviors. In many cases, smoking was probably a more surreptitious activity when not socially sanctioned. Only in the last century have women been able to smoke openly without risking public scorn. It is another story altogether that smoking is looked down upon in the more "smoke-free" climate of twenty-first-century America.

Tobacco in the West

In the western settlement of late-nineteenth- and early twentieth-century America, social contexts were different. In the hinterlands of the American West, smoking in public was not as subservient to the dictates of late Victorian strictures. Ideas of liberalism and individuality came fully into play in the wide-open spaces. As Mary Douglas and Baron Isherwood (1996: 20–21) explain, individuality tends to emerge where groups are ephemeral or less important. Although it could be argued that groups influence those who wish to express their uniqueness, in places like saloons and even the U.S. Cavalry it was essentially every individual for himself or herself, in the sense that the group mentality was at times less pervasive in the cultural milieu of the West.

Whether out of need or as a form of sociability, tobacco played an integral role in ideas of individuality and in the settlement of the western frontier, as illustrated by two case studies. The first, by Shannon Vihlene (2008), involves the use of tobacco by the Seventh Cavalry in coping with the anxieties of a military campaign in Montana and the ensuing tragic events that unfolded at the Battle of Little Bighorn. The second draws on Kelly Dixon's superb study (2005) of four saloon sites in Virginia City, Nevada.

Custer's Last Drag

Life on the American frontier was fraught with alternating spells of danger and boredom, punctuated by fear and excitement. Against this backdrop of anxiety, people used tobacco as a means to comfort themselves in times of stress. One particular case stands out in this regard—the use of tobacco in June 1876 by the Seventh Cavalry, stationed at Little Bighorn in the wilds of Montana. In a study by Shannon Vihlene (personal communication, June 7, 2011), evidence of tobacco use among officers and soldiers is clear. Vihlene addresses the prevalence of tobacco usage in nineteenth-century America in her research, paying special attention to the use of tobacco by the American military.

By studying markers on the human skeletal remains excavated from the Little Bighorn battlefield in the 1984–1985 and 1992 excavations at the Custer National Cemetery (originally studied by Scott and Snow 1991; Scott and Willey 1997; and Scott et al. 1998), Vihlene was able to determine that tobacco was heavily used by the soldiers. The most reliable evidence comes from inspecting the dental remains of Seventh Cavalry soldiers to evaluate dental attrition, dental staining, and pipe-stem abrasion grooves in the teeth in order to compare it to Army Muster Rolls and the documentation of sales of tobacco rations issued by the U.S. military (Willey and Scott 1999: 661; Vihlene 2008: 2, 33).

Markers on teeth suggest tobacco usage, including smooth polishing and hard concave abrasions produced by smoking clay tobacco pipes. Both clay pipes and chewing tobacco can also result in an exostosis, which is a bony growth produced by the continual contraction of the temporalis muscle. This constant contraction, caused by clenching a pipe in the teeth or constant mastication of tobacco, could lead to ossification at the point of muscle attachment to the temporal line in the human skull (Vihlene 2008: 32; Willey 1997: 43). One set of skeletal remains was identified as belonging to Mitch Boyer, of mixed ancestry, the scout for the Custer battalion. Upon examination, Boyer's teeth revealed dental abrasions from pipe smoking (Scott et al. 1998: 80–81; Fox et al. 2000: 80). Willey et al. (1996: 10–12) observe that most of the analyzed dentition showed tobacco use in various forms (mostly by chewing and pipe smoking) in addition to dental abrasions. Staining can be seen in the form of dark brown or black discolorations from tar and chew-

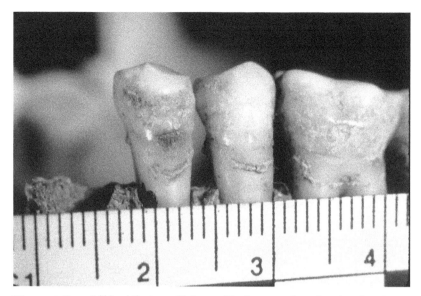

Figure 16. Buccal ("cheek") view of left mandibular premolars showing abrasion on their occlusal surfaces consistent with alterations expected of habitual use of a clay pipe stem. Custer National Cemetery Burial 8B, Grave 517A. These bones might possibly be George Custer's, although he eschewed tobacco use according to historic accounts; there are also other inconsistencies between the skeleton and accounts of Custer. Courtesy of P. Willey.

ing tobacco on the lingual surface of the tooth, which comes in contact with the tongue (Willey 1997: 107; Vihlene 2008: 6–8). Willey et al. (1996: 11) also note that Custer prohibited smoking in the final days of the campaign to avoid detection, so the soldiers resorted to chewing before their deaths. Figures 16 and 17 indicate examples of dental wear and staining from the Seventh Cavalry at Little Bighorn.

When comparing the dental evidence with the archival evidence, the argument for heavy tobacco usage among the Seventh Cavalry and the American military as a whole is compelling. Vihlene (2008: 43) reports that tobacco consumption for the average individual in 1880 was 3.2 pounds. In contrast, consumption in the U.S. Army was 10.9 pounds per person. Additionally, even though American soldiers had to pay for their tobacco rations, the purchase of tobacco remained a priority among other pressing and necessary expenses (Vihlene 2008: 42). Even if a soldier did not smoke or chew tobacco, it could always be used as a form of currency for gambling, barter, and other

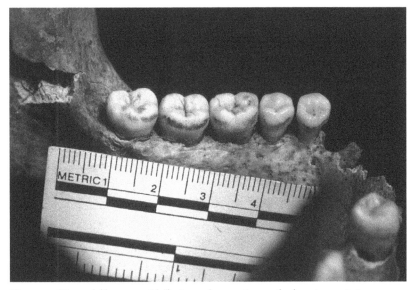

Figure 17. Lingual ("tongue-side") view of posterior teeth showing staining consistent with tobacco use. The dentist who examined the teeth (Richard Glenner) identified the deposits as most likely caused by pipe smoking. Custer National Cemetery Burial 7. Courtesy of P. Willey.

activities (Vihlene 2008: 45). Vihlene (2008: 51) notes that many soldiers who did use tobacco preferred chewing tobacco to smoking.

Shannon Vilhene raises interesting questions about tobacco use in the U.S. Army. Why was tobacco use so prevalent among the American military and especially soldiers at Little Bighorn? Given the uncertainty of life and death on the frontier, tobacco use makes sense. Quoting Joseph Robert (1967), Vihlene (2008: 46–47) offers several possibilities. First, smoking and chewing tobacco provided a coping mechanism in dealing with the stresses of military life during wartime. Second, it seems likely that soldiers would prefer using tobacco when free from the constraints of their families. Finally, in the collective consciousness of soldiers on the frontier, young men were more likely to mimic their peers and superiors by adopting smoking. Vihlene (2008: 47) observes that life in the military, not "known for its morality or cohesiveness," fostered drinking, smoking, and other vices. Using tobacco on the frontier probably arose more from necessity than from choice. Tobacco, after all, was the salve of the everyday soldier living on the edge of the American wilderness, a world of the uncertain and the unknowable.

Boomtown Saloons

In her groundbreaking work *The Legacy of Conquest: The Unbroken Past of the American West*, historian Patricia Limerick (1987) helped to dispel some of the stereotypes and myths of the "wild West," demonstrating that the West was a place of great complexity, dynamic borders, and ethnic diversity. Her work and the scholarship of other western historians have influenced a generation of historical archaeologists. Recent research in historical archaeology bears this out, such as the insightful *Boomtown Saloons* by archaeologist Kelly Dixon (2005), based on the archaeological excavations of several saloon sites in Virginia City, Nevada.

In this scenario, we are treated to the fascinating realities of the West, where the enjoyment of tobacco once again demonstrates the importance as well as the ubiquity of tobacco consumption and its role in the myth-busting of saloon life. Archaeological evidence comes from four saloons: the Boston Saloon, an African American establishment; the Hibernia Brewery; Piper's Old Corner Bar; and O'Brien and Costello's Saloon and Shooting Gallery.

Dixon (2005: 112, 148) observes that the three most common forms of entertainment (or vices) in Virginia City and other boomtowns were drinking, smoking, and gambling, which usually went hand in hand as pleasant and welcome diversions from the privations of a hard life. Further archaeological evidence for tobacco-related activities at the Virginia City excavations included one red clay pipe bowl, "TD" pipes, and three stoneware spittoons recovered from Piper's Old Corner Bar (Dixon 2005: 117–20). One of the more curious finds was a meerschaum pipe bowl recovered from Piper's Old Corner Bar that was elaborately decorated with a hunting motif. Because the mineral sepiolite (a hydrous magnesium silicate) is generally found only in the Eskisehir region of Turkey, such hand-carved pipes were considered higher-end and were smoked only by those who could afford them. Was John Piper, the owner, someone who discovered newfound wealth in the mining boom, and could this have been his very own pipe (Dixon 2005: 117)?

In any case, Dixon (2005: 114) found that white clay tobacco pipes were the most common type of smoking paraphernalia recovered at the four saloons with their varying clientele. The Boston Saloon stood out for the greatest quantity of clay pipes and related tobacco-smoking equipment (Dixon 2005: 114).

Some of the more unusual finds included three undecorated red clay pipe bowls in the shape of a "J" as well as a red clay pipe bowl distinctive for its two parallel bands. The origins of these pipes remain unknown (Dixon 2005: 115). In addition, two ceramic spittoons were found, indicating another way in which tobacco was consumed (Dixon 2005: 119–20).

Perhaps one of the most exciting discoveries was an amber pipe stem mouthpiece with clench marks. The pipe was excavated from the Hibernia Brewery site (Dixon 2005: 117). DNA analysis from the areas of the tooth marks reveals that the pipe was smoked by a woman, as indicated by the presence of two X chromosomes. This reinforces the perception that women openly smoked in the more rural areas of the country (Dixon 2005: 144–45). More importantly, this finding, corroborated by a number of artifacts, implies a female presence in Virginia City saloons. The artifacts include glass buttons from women's shoes, buttons reflecting Victorian clothing styles, and small glass beads (Dixon 2005: 124–32). Whether these represent items belonging to prostitutes, saloon workers, actual saloon owners, such as Amanda Payne, or possible patrons at the more upscale Boston Saloon will never be known. But they do present evidentiary challenges to the gender-bias in stereotypes of the "Old West" (Dixon 2005: 145).

The collective material culture of saloon life in Virginia City, in contrast to the gun-toting, swaggering Hollywood stereotypes, indicates far more complexity on the frontier. Dixon's excavations reveal glimpses into multi-ethnic and possibly gender-related dimensions of life experienced in western boomtowns (Schablitsky 2007: 194–95). Saloons, rather than being places of violence and conflict, were likely places of social refuge for the ethnically diverse communities who inhabited these towns. The saloon provided the space to relax over a drink, a smoke, and possibly a game of dice or cards to pass the time in a place that offered few distractions and much time to speculate (Dixon 2005: 157–59).

Houses of Sin: Tobacco and Brothels

Studies of saloons and public venues that cater to "pleasures of the flesh" have contributed to the growing interest in the archaeology of spaces that have routinely been stereotyped in the media. The historical archaeology of brothels is beginning to reveal a growing body of material data that does not easily fit into preconceived notions of nineteenth-century prostitution. Rather, the archaeology of prostitution covers a gamut of research interests from feminism to status and class. Brothels can also represent consumer choice for both the inhabitants of brothels and their clientele.

As Anne-Marie Cantwell and Diana Wall (2001: 220) observe, prostitution served either as a means of survival or to supplement desperately needed income among working-class women in nineteenth-century New York. In fact, it may have been the most lucrative profession, although not without its dangers and sometimes tragic outcomes. Madams had the best of the situation, occupying one of the very few managerial/entrepreneurial positions that a woman could hold at that time (Cantwell and Wall 2001: 221; Hill 1993: 64–73).

In Donna Seifert's study of brothels (1991), she compares artifact assemblages from a brothel in the ethnically diverse Washington, D.C., neighborhood historically known as Hooker's Division to working-class household assemblages from two other Washington, D.C., neighborhoods. Seifert discovers different consumer patterns in terms of household composition and function, suggesting that women in the more upscale brothels often fared better than their working-class counterparts (Seifert 1991: 93–94). All three assemblages included clay tobacco pipes, the greatest number being recovered from the brothel. Seifert (1991: 100) attributes this to men's frequent visitation of the brothels, where drinking, smoking, and eating were more common pastimes when compared to working-class households. More significantly, although the women in all three neighborhoods were working women and probably all of working-class backgrounds, Seifert (1991: 103–4) concludes that the artifact assemblages from the households reflect homemaker activities of families on a tight budget. This contrasts starkly with the businesslike nature of the brothel, where consumer choices reflected the residents and madam, while the tobacco pipes represent the consumer choice of the male customers.

During the construction of the Smithsonian's National Museum of the American Indian on the National Mall in Washington, D.C., a high-class brothel known as Mary Ann Hall's brothel was located. A study by Donna Seifert and Joseph Balicki (2005) compared the brothel in Hooker's Division to Mary Ann Hall's establishment and found differences. For example, the Mary Ann Hall site had far fewer clay tobacco pipes. Seifert and Balicki

(2005: 63, 65) suggest that this could represent a preference for cigarettes beginning during this period. They are careful to note, however, that they saw no single pattern or artifact signature in comparing Washington, D.C., brothels: "brothel assemblages are peculiar, but they are peculiar in different ways for different time periods and economic classes" (Seifert and Balicki 2005: 71). Consequently, sex for cash was carried out in a number of settings in turn-of-the-century America. These included cribs (simple and unadorned single rooms opening to a street or back alley); rooms above saloons; and high-end brothels and parlor houses operated by well-to-do madams (Meyer, Gibson, and Costello 2005: 109; Spude 2005: 90).

Catherine Spude (2005) makes a similar observation for brothels in the West. In comparing eight artifact assemblages from mining-related communities, Spude (2005) maintains that saloons and brothels served similar purposes for working-class customers, the chief difference being that consumer choice for these establishments was predicated on gender. To encourage sociability, however, the establishments had similarities, such as the availability of liquor and sex for sale at both. As Spude (2005: 91) observes, "for archaeologists, the principal difference between the saloons and brothels was not so much what occurred behind the swinging doors but, rather, who selected the material culture: men or women." This was partly dictated by the prohibition of women as customers in saloons, either by law or by social convention, leaving them little or no choice in saloons, unlike brothels, which were predominantly the domain of women (Spude 2005: 91).

After examining artifact collections from Alaska, Colorado, Alberta, Canada, and Los Angeles, California, Spude (2005: 98–99, 102) found that tobacco-related items, mostly in the form of pipes, in the saloon and brothel assemblages were almost identical and could be linked to a male presence in both types of establishments. When compared to assemblages at residences in these mining communities, the family households had fewer tobacco-related items than the saloons and brothels. Spude (2005: 102) attributes this to aspects of respectability: women in family households may have suppressed tobacco use in their homes, unlike men who could freely indulge their smoking habit in accepted social spaces (Spude 2005: 99). In assessing the nearly identical findings for tobacco and smoking-related activity in both saloons and brothels, Spude (2005: 102) suggests that this reflects the nature of these institutions as places where "women indulged men . . . in partaking of bodily pleasures in that age of repressed middle-class sensuality, [where] sex, intoxicating drink, tobacco, all were available for the pleasure of the customer."

Conclusion

What can be said about the role that tobacco played in the American experience? Tobacco's place in American life has been as varied as the people who have utilized it, whether related to religious ritual, comfort, relaxation and pleasure, boredom and anxiety, trade and diplomacy, power relations, defiance, or identity formation and solidarity. Tobacco and smoking, as viewed through the lens of historical archaeology, can be seen as a conduit to understanding the lives of those who had little or no voice in the official records.

The uses of the material culture of tobacco pipes and related paraphernalia in varied contexts and meanings provide a window into the lives of Native Americans, explorers, colonists, laborers, and many others whose voices have been suppressed, overlooked, or ignored. Spanning centuries of use, tobacco pipes and the simple act of smoking have been laden with multiple meanings. Through the study of tobacco and smoking, the archaeologist is presented with the chance to interpret evidence from a body of data that, when combined with the tools of ethnohistorical information and scientific archaeology, is at once both powerful and enlightening.

Here we are able to see how people intelligently and creatively adapted to changing circumstances and dramatic events over which they often had little control. For Native Americans, the indigenous plant offered a way to negotiate, maintain peaceful relations, trade, and celebrate. During the Contact Period, tobacco enhanced communication, serving as a means to transcend the often seemingly strange and at times offensive manners of white strangers who made incomprehensible demands in the ordered sphere of Native American checks and balances, based on formal gift exchange and kin relationships. At a time of great flux and change, tobacco may have proved instrumental to indigenous coping strategies by providing spiritual substance when faced with escalating disruption and chaos.

Once Europeans discovered tobacco's usefulness as well as its potency as a stimulant, they adopted it with an unprecedented zeal. Tobacco became a dominant agricultural product that helped establish the American colonies on the Eastern Seaboard. The astounding archaeological evidence of thousands of clay tobacco pipes recovered from colonial sites testifies to a deeply ingrained habit in the colonists' everyday lives. They used it as both a lifeline and a part of their lifestyle, even to the detriment of their own health.

We do not know for certain whether enslaved Africans produced their own clay pipes for personal use and identity affirmation or the role that tobacco played beyond the act of smoking. But tobacco was inescapably integrated into their lives through the mechanisms of the colonial tobacco complex. Perhaps future research in historical archaeology will shed light on tobacco use among enslaved Africans in North America and the Caribbean. Much remains to be done in this area.

While tobacco and smoking offered a pastime that everyone could share as part of the American experience, they also reinforced boundaries along lines of status, class, and ethnicity. For textile mill workers, urban Irish immigrants, and the leisurely classes, tobacco provided a means of self-expression and identity. Whether a middle-class female smoker concealed her habit behind closed doors or Irish Americans proudly displayed their political affiliations though insignia on clay pipes, tobacco was ever present during the transition from a more rural and agricultural way of life to the realities introduced by the Industrial Revolution and urbanization.

In fact, when examining major transitions in American life, tobacco has always been there, offering a way to make the changes more palatable. Isolated on the western frontier, bored and anxious soldiers used and traded tobacco for pleasure and power. Ritualized acts of smoking and drinking in saloons and brothels allowed for escape from the harsh rough and tumble of mining towns and makeshift settlements prone to uncertain futures. Although smoking tobacco may have provided solace in the face of anxiety, it also served as something enjoyable and pleasurable, accompanied by drink and good company.

In the American experience, stimulants like tobacco helped people to cope with the daily challenges ushered in by the forces of modernity, capitalism, and industrialization, propelling a young nation toward the unknown. In a world characterized by contradictory democratic freedoms and social restrictions, citizens could challenge the status quo, test novel ideas, and form identities, all while carving out their niche in what would become a place that was and is uniquely American. Throughout these times, tobacco helped smooth the journey, brighten the day, and soothe the soul.

Despite all of the endeavors surrounding tobacco and smoking, however, Native Americans are to be credited not only for introducing the plant to Europeans but for utilizing tobacco in a number of significant ways. Long before Europeans first stepped foot on American soil, indigenous peoples were smoking, rolling, and absorbing tobacco. Archaeologically, tobacco smoking among Native North Americans is most manifest in the use of calumet or stone pipes. Such practices were later documented by explorers, traders, colonists, and ethnographers.

Indian communities demonstrate a variety of uses for tobacco, from shamanistic rituals, relaxation, and ceremonies to diplomacy, gift exchanges, and trade. The importance of the greeting ritual and the use of tobacco smoking as a political activity cannot be underestimated in the complex developments during the formation of the Iroquois League in the Late Woodland period.

During the Contact Period, French fur traders and explorers realized the importance of the "symbolic armor" of the calumet pipe. Their efforts toward establishing trade relations with indigenous peoples relied exclusively upon the very specific roles and etiquette of the Calumet Ceremony, which acted as a ritual of encounter. Native Americans, for their part, needed to establish fictive kin relations in order to legitimize these interactions with each other and with European intruders.

Perhaps the greatest irony in the history of tobacco and smoking, however, is the transculturation process of tobacco through human contact then appropriation and finally reintroduction. This began with the introduction of tobacco by Native Americans to Europeans in the mid-fifteenth century, followed by the European adoption of tobacco and then its reintroduction as a commodity to Indian communities through trade and gift exchange. In a sense, the entire process underlies what would form the basis of a capitalist world system, which is explored in the next chapter.

6

A Pipe-Lover's Dream

Port Royal, Jamaica, and Early Tobacco Use in British America

Once reputed to be the "wickedest city in the world," Port Royal, Jamaica, typifies the consumer revolution of the early modern period. As a lively port in the seventeenth-century English Caribbean, Port Royal had every kind of imaginable commodity available as shiploads of goods came and went. Firkins (barrels) of butter and other foodstuffs, spirits, Chinese porcelain, and expertly crafted pewter plates, tankards, and utensils filled the holds of westbound vessels hailing from London, Liverpool, and Bristol. The supply of alcohol, tobacco, and luxury goods was not only continuous but necessary to occupy and entertain the town's citizens and visitors alike. Given the scarcity of fresh water, rum, ale, and other spirits were normal fare, while tobacco smoking was a fact of life. Everyone smoked. The chief items in the cargo of incoming ships were thousands of white clay tobacco pipes, crammed into large hogsheads bursting at the seams.

A quick assessment of the clay tobacco pipe collection from Port Royal verifies this state of affairs and attests to the popularity of smoking. Over the course of ten years of archaeological excavation (from 1981 to 1990) directed by Dr. Donny Hamilton, 21,575 clay pipe remains were found. This collection is regarded as one of the largest clay tobacco pipe collections archaeologically recovered in the Americas and therefore can provide a window into the *Zeitgeist* of underlying social and economic transitions of the early modern era. In many respects, Port Royal exemplified these changes. On one hand, a Caribbean colony like Port Royal was a microcosm of London, maintaining English cultural values and identity; but on the other, this New World colony reflected the shifting tides of novel freedoms, anxieties, and newly emerging habits.

Located at the southernmost portion of the southeast section of Jamaica, Port Royal is a small sandspit jutting thumb-like into Kingston Harbor. In 1655 the town was well positioned to see who was coming and going along the Caribbean Sea lanes and Spanish Main. Languishing as a Spanish outpost, the island was seized by the English without much difficulty in 1655, after an unsuccessful attempt to seize neighboring Hispaniola (Pawson and Buisseret 2000: 7). As in most English settlements, a fort was quickly established. With its deep-water harbor and safe anchorage, Port Royal was a true coup in English long-term colonization efforts. Once it was fortified, Port Royal's advantageous location prompted merchants, sea captains, craftspeople, and immigrants to grace its shores as it became the most economically successful English port in the Americas, flourishing until its devastation by a powerful earthquake shortly before noon on June 7, 1692 (Hamilton 1992: 40).

Port Royal fits well within the parameters of Wallerstein's world-systems analysis. As an English colony, Port Royal's export trade in raw materials included tobacco and sugar as well as cargo in small exotics such as pimento, indigo, and cacao nuts (Pawson and Buisseret 2000: 85–86, 91). Inbound ships brought everything from foodstuffs to furniture, window glass, bricks, arms, mass quantities of alcohol, naval stores, ceramics, and a host of other items to outfit the colony in style (Pawson and Buisseret 2000: 89). The general character and cultural flavor of the town was influenced by the influx of English buccaneers and privateers from the island of Tortuga in 1657. Invited to deposit their plunder in Port Royal's coffers, they accepted. The offer was rescinded in 1680, when buccaneers were considered "a nuisance" (Pawson and Buisseret 2000: 44). By then it was moot, as Port Royal had been fully colonized. Given the fascination with pirates, much has been made of this period of Port Royal's history, but most of it is sensational and overblown, obscuring the more interesting aspects of the town's history.

What is remarkable about Port Royal is the lightning-speed growth of the port. For example, in 1668 about 800 houses dotted the tiny sandspit; by 1692 the town occupied 51 acres inhabited by approximately 6,500 residents and 2,000 buildings, many constructed of imported bricks brought over as ballast on ships (Hamilton 1992: 40; Pawson and Buisseret 2000: 135–36; Taylor 1965: 135). Even by modern standards, Port Royal was high density: its streets were tightly packed with buildings and people and flanked by a lively waterfront crammed with outdoor markets. Henry Barham (1722: 177), an English medical doctor, noted that the streets were "very Regular and the Houses Built with Brick and beautiful with Balconies after the Modern Way of Building in London."

Port Royal was also home to a diverse mix of immigrants from Barbados, Bermuda, New England, and the British Isles. Inhabitants came from all walks of life and social classes, including families with children, merchants, various craftspeople, indentured servants, prostitutes, and a transient population of privateers, sea captains, sailors, and smugglers. Africans were brought in by ship to work the plantations in the island's interior. Some remained free in Port Royal, while others were not so fortunate (Taylor 1965: 134). Economic historian Nuala Zahedieh (1986: 220) estimates that by 1680 Port Royal was possibly clearing 150 to 200 vessels a year. Significantly, the archaeological evidence supports this hypothesis in terms of the sheer quantities of both necessities and luxury goods. As the Caribbean's busiest port, Port Royal was one of the chief bastions of financial opportunity for enterprising merchants, sea captains, and traders (Taylor 1965: 134). This segment of the population really constituted the true nature of Port Royal, as opposed to pirates. This had far-reaching implications. About five hundred merchants at Port Royal financed many of the island's plantations between 1664 and 1700. The wealth of these merchants derived primarily from the sale of import commodities and allowed them to exercise influence over the town (Scammell 1989: 13; Zahedieh 1986: 221). They were Port Royal's elite and middling classes, whose presence shaped the daily lives of the town's inhabitants and the immigrant experience.

Like other English colonies, Port Royal offered a haven for those desiring a fresh start in the New World. It was a time of newly forged identities and experimentation. Enormous fortunes were made from smuggling and the acquisition of vast tracts of land in the island's interior, creating a powerful planter class in addition to the merchants. Some complained bitterly about the beneficiaries of this newfound wealth, who were considered to be "formerly rude and mean of birth" (Scammell 1989: 179). In a classic New World rags to riches story, Peter Beckford typified the Port Royal rise of the merchant and planter classes. Although a man of modest means upon his arrival in 1661, Beckford left behind an estate worth millions by today's standards by the time he died in 1710, with 20 plantations and 1,200 slaves to his name (Scammell 1989: 179).

Most importantly, the desire for imported luxury goods on the part of the wealthy planters and merchants not only encouraged active commerce but also guaranteed the availability of a wide range of items to help ensure comfort, demonstrate prosperity, and maintain links to the home country. Through comfort, the material world of luxury goods reinforced English values and identity, while it encouraged the development of pastimes and practices that introduced new modes of interaction and lifestyles. The probate inventories, shipping records, and archaeological evidence confirm these developments. The remains of crystal drinking glasses, pewter dinnerware, silver eating utensils, Chinese porcelain, and other fine ceramics all testify to the variety of trade goods and consumer tastes within the realm of a preindustrial consumerism (as discussed later in this chapter). Packed among such goods in the holds of ships were the barrels and boxes of thousands of clay tobacco pipes. These rather plain and ubiquitous objects dulled in comparison with the more illustrious consumables, but their arrival was eagerly anticipated.

The Evidence for Smoking at Port Royal

The Archaeological Evidence

Just how common was smoking at Port Royal? Valuable clues were found at the intersection of Queen and Lime Streets, the commercial heart of the town, where the greatest concentrations of pipes were excavated (figure 18). The majority of pipes recovered from Port Royal fall within the range of occupation, from Port Royal's founding in 1655 to the 1692 earthquake, although very few pipes in the collection date to the early days of the town. The site also contains pipes that postdate the earthquake. Port Royal was not completely abandoned after the earthquake and, with the addition of the British Naval Hospital in 1817, operated well into the early twentieth century (Pawson and Buisseret 2000: 193, 200). This accounts for a scattering of nineteenth-century pipes that appear stratigraphically above the occupation

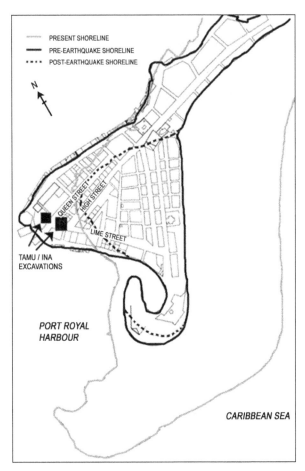

PRESENT SHORELINE
PRE-EARTHQUAKE SHORELINE
POST-EARTHQUAKE SHORELINE

N

QUEEN STREET

HIGH STREET

LIME STREET

TAMU / INA
EXCAVATIONS

PORT ROYAL
HARBOUR

CARIBBEAN SEA

Figure 18. Intersection of Lime and Queen Streets, Port Royal, Jamaica, where archaeological excavations were conducted by Donny L. Hamilton from 1981 to 1990. Courtesy of the Port Royal Project, Department of Anthropology, Texas A&M University.

layer. A small assemblage of red clay pipes (discussed in chapter 4) was also found. The stem diameters of six Dutch clay pipes cannot be dated, so these pipes were not included as part of the main analysis. In sum, all pipes included in the study were seen as representing the entire collection. But pipes were clearly designated by stratigraphic deposition, so that the occupation layer was delineated from later periods. The red clay and Dutch pipes were not included in the final analysis.

The archaeological contexts for the pipes encompass the entire site, but specific clusters and patterns can be discerned. The majority of pipes appeared in three main areas: Building 1, Building 3, and Building 4/5. Building 1 (figure 19), where the largest collection of clay pipes was found (6,894 pipes), was a substantial brick building with six ground-floor rooms divided

Figure 19. Well-preserved floor and fallen timber from Building 1, Port Royal, Jamaica. Courtesy of the Port Royal Project, Department of Anthropology, Texas A&M University.

into three separate two-room combinations. These rooms appear to have been used as a wine/pipe shop, a tavern, and a combination wood turner/cobbler's shop, representing a multifunctional building. With regard to the assemblage of recovered pipes, 48 percent had been smoked, indicating that pipe smoking was a common activity. The remainder had never been smoked, probably representing retail stock sold to customers in the tavern and wine/pipe shop (Hamilton 1984: 21, 1985: 105, 1986: 74, 1992: 44).

Building 3 (figure 20), whose function is unknown, appears to have included a storage area, with over five thousand unused white clay tobacco pipes as well as corked and monogrammed wine bottles and various measuring scales and weights that possibly related to activities in nearby buildings and were used for a nearby outdoor market (Hamilton 1988: 9, personal communication, 1997). Building 4/5, which yielded over 3,500 clay pipes, produced the richest array of material culture for artifacts recovered in situ. These included (but were not limited to) two sets of Chinese porcelain Fo Dogs, almost thirty Chinese porcelain cups and bowls, a large number of pewter plates, candlesticks, an English tin-glazed vase, a brass mortar, a dec-

Figure 20. Underwater image shows scattered unsmoked clay pipes in situ in Building 3, which were probably meant for retail sale in the shops and taverns of Port Royal, Jamaica. Courtesy of the Port Royal Project, Department of Anthropology, Texas A&M University.

Figure 21. Artifacts recovered from underwater archaeological excavations at Port Royal, Jamaica. Courtesy of the Port Royal Project, Department of Anthropology, Texas A&M University.

orated Dutch Delft plate, a gold ring, and silver forks and spoons (figure 21; Hamilton 1991, 2000).

The building consisted of at least six rooms, several of which appear to have been associated with entertaining, food preparation, and service to patrons, along with hearths and yards used as outdoor food preparation and multiuse areas. Building 4 is a possible residence-accommodation, perhaps for the servants and slaves who worked in Building 5. Building 5 may have served as a victualing house or a restaurant in more modern parlance. Most of the pipes found in the building complex were recovered from the yard areas, especially Yard 4A/4B (1,795 pipes). Many had been smoked (1,487 pipes) and were found in contexts with refuse, such as butchered animal bone (Hamilton 1990: 14).

Pipe Distribution Patterns and South's Brunswick Pattern of Disposal

Provenience and context are the sine qua non of archaeological investigation. In the case of Port Royal, the study of the distribution of clay tobacco pipes not only helped determine room and building function but also contributed to understanding the contexts in which pipes were stored, sold, and smoked as well as how their disposable nature manifested itself on Port Royal's landscape. As possibly the first real mass-produced disposable commodity of the early modern era, clay pipe refuse arouses interest.

As Stanley South (1977, 1978) emphasizes, recognizing the patterns of artifact distributions on archaeological sites is essential to archaeological reasoning and the interpretation of human behavior. South's distinguishing of clay tobacco pipes as a separate group of artifacts in pattern recognition is worth noting, particularly in regard to their wide variability (South 1977: 96–97, 106). South's Brunswick Pattern of Refuse Disposal, as he proposes in *Method and Theory in Historical Archaeology*, provides a type of repetitive disposal behavior that can be used to predict refuse deposits on British colonial sites (South 1977: 47). South's excavations at Brunswick Town, North Carolina, revealed a distinct and consistent pattern produced by its eighteenth-century occupants whereby rubbish was discarded adjacent to the structures, specifically at the front and back doors of the dwellings (South 1977: 47). Where did Port Royal's residents toss their easily disposable used pipes after they smoked them, especially in a town that offered high-density living on a tiny sandspit? To determine whether the Brunswick Pattern was applicable to the clay pipe distributions at Port Royal, an analysis was conducted.

From the outset, two distinct clusters of clay pipes were found at Port Royal for Level 3, the occupation period. The first appeared as concentrations of new pipes inside Buildings 1 and 3. These were the pipes that were to be sold in the taverns, restaurants, and shops at Port Royal. The provenience of the used (smoked) pipes was another story. The best evidence for this behavior comes from the yards of Building 4/5, which was probably of mixed use but indicates an outdoor kitchen and food preparation area. Only 334 pipes were found inside, in contrast to the large accumulation of smoked and broken pipes associated with *all* of the yards, totaling 2,019 pipes (Fox 1999). For the Brunswick Pattern, South (1977: 48) states: "On British-American sites of the eighteenth century a concentrated refuse deposit will be found at the points of entrance and exit in dwellings, shops, and military fortifications."

For example, South indicated that the clay pipes and wine bottles formed a major concentration in a yard area of the Public House–Tailor Shop at Brunswick Town and at the rear of the structure, not far from the kitchen (South 1977: 71). In examining the correlation of clay pipes to activity areas around the Drax Hall Great House in Jamaica, Douglas Armstrong (1990: 265, 131) reports that only one pipe was recovered in the wall foundations of the house, compared to 97.9 percent of the clay pipe remains found in the nearby planter's kitchen refuse area, which was downslope from the kitchen. In this case, the Brunswick Pattern may or may not be conclusive. In contrast, at the Country's House Site at St. Mary's City, Maryland, large accumulations of refuse were discovered immediately adjacent to the front and back doors of the building. In fact, this pattern persisted throughout the seventeenth century, regardless of the building's functions, as it changed from a private residence to a public inn (Miller 1994: 66, 74, 80).

These few examples demonstrate the variety in disposal behavior and raise the question as to how applicable the Brunswick Pattern is to some British colonial sites or even within specific areas of a given site. The interpretations of the distribution patterns at Port Royal, as they relate to the Brunswick Pattern, are mixed. For Buildings 1 and 3 the pattern does not apply, as most of the clay pipes were found inside; the other accumulated refuse for those buildings reflects multiple activities rather than the refuse behavior associated with the Brunswick Pattern. It is open to interpretation as to whether the Brunswick Pattern can be clearly identified for the Building 4/5 complex, however, because the yards were multiuse areas, including food preparation. The Brunswick Pattern indicates a worldview that was informal and communal, where untidy yards were accepted and tolerated (Deetz 1977: 39–40; Miller 1994: 81). In the case of Port Royal, however, this behavior was less likely, simply because the town was so tightly compacted and crowded that the yards provided important areas of extended work space (figure 22). The significant amounts of clay pipes in the outdoor areas may suggest that used and smoked pipes were thrown in the rubbish pile with other refuse, including butchered bone and broken ceramics, which was all then promptly buried in the backyard, clearing out and making available precious work space.

Figure 22. Oliver Cox's map of Port Royal, Jamaica, showing the high density of the town. Courtesy of the Port Royal Project, Department of Anthropology, Texas A&M University.

The Port Royal Typology

The first purpose of creating a typology for the Port Royal pipes was to provide a typology for English clay pipes that would be useful to other archaeologists in their research. The second reason was to ascertain whether discernible trends in styles emerged over time and might reflect consumer demand. After a long and painstaking process, a typology of sixty-one distinct pipe types was finally established. Because pipe bowls became larger as tobacco prices fell and bowl shapes changed over time in many instances, clay tobacco pipe typologies are usually based on *bowl* types, which was the case for the Port Royal pipes. Other characteristics such as heels were considered, but only after bowl types were firmly determined in the development of the Port Royal typology.

The first attempt as classifying English clay tobacco pipes was in 1951 by Adrian Oswald (Oswald 1959), whose initial work was aided by the histogram of James C. Harrington (1954), which provided relative date ranges. In a stroke of pure genius, Harrington applied a set of drill bits to measure the stem diameter of archaeologically recovered clay pipes from his work at Colonial Jamestown. As tobacco prices dropped and tobacco became affordable, Harrington realized, the size of the clay pipe bowls increased to accommodate more tobacco, resulting in longer stems with smaller bore hole diameters. As bowl size increased, a longer stem with a smaller bore hole had three main functions. First, a longer stem provided a longer channel to draw the smoke properly. Second, because a larger bowl held more tobacco, a smaller bore and bore hole could act as a filter to avoid inhaling bits of tobacco. Finally, the smaller bore also kept loose tobacco and ash from clogging up the stem bore. Still, this was no guarantee: one pipe recovered from Port Royal has a small stone lodged at the opening of the bore in the bowl; whether this was intentional to prevent bits of tobacco and ash from funneling through the pipe's stem bore remains a mystery.

Harrington used drill bits that measured in sixty-fourths of an inch to measure the stem diameters, beginning with 9/64 for the largest and earliest dated pipes, to 4/64 for later dates. From this Harrington developed his highly useful histogram, which was later refined in 1962 by Lewis Binford, who applied an algorithm to test the date ranges for greater accuracy (Harrington 1954; Binford 1962). Because Port Royal has a statistically large sample size and a known date of the 1692 earthquake, this provided a good

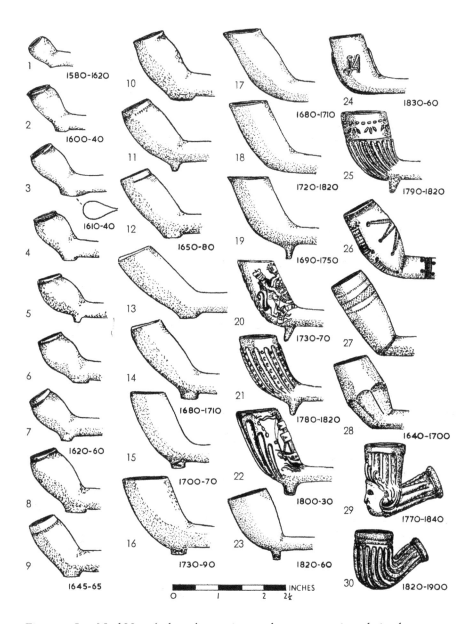

Figure 23. Ivor Noël Hume's clay tobacco pipe typology, representing relative date ranges for clay pipes manufactured from 1580 to 1900. From *A Guide to Artifacts of Colonial America* by Ivor Noël Hume (1969). Used by permission of Alfred A. Knopf, an imprint of the Knopf Doubleday Publishing group, a Division of Random House, LLC.

opportunity to test the accuracy of pipe-stem dating for Level 3, the occupation layer, and to compare the Harrington/Binford method to the one proposed by Robert Heighton and Kathleen Deagan (1971). After testing, the Harrington/Binford typology date ranges showed greater consistency, with an accuracy of four to seven years, whereas the Heighton/Deagan method produced dates off by twenty years or more. Dates ranged from 1718 to 1723, as compared to the Harrington/Binford method, which produced dates between 1685 and 1696, yielding a mean of 1692.3, as tested against the *terminus ante quem* of 1692 (Fox 1999).

Ivor Noël Hume (1969: 302–4) offered one of the most helpful clay tobacco pipe typologies in historical archaeology, which created the basis for the Port Royal typology (figure 23). Consulting *Archaeological Typology and Practical Reality: A Dialectical Approach to Artifact Classification and Sorting* (Adams and Adams 2007) was very helpful in the whole process. After the typology was completed, it was time to see if any distinct patterns emerged. The first pattern was where certain pipe types appeared at the site. The most common bowl forms were represented by clusters of new, unsmoked pipes found in Room 5 of Building 1 and Room 2 of Building 3. This is probably because the greatest number of pipes came from these buildings, where pipes to be sold in Port Royal were stored.

Following that trend, the typology also revealed sixty-one types in all, based on bowl shape and size. They could be further broken down into four main categories based on the bowl shape and style: forty-six bowl types had flat heels, seven bowl types had spurs, three bowl types had no heels (heel-less export pipes), and five outliers did not fit into any particular category. Heels on pipes do not seem to indicate any particular trend. According to Oswald (1959: 59), heel-less pipes were more likely to be exported to the American colonies because they were less prone to breakage during shipment than those with flat heels and spurs. The number of heel-less pipes in comparison to pipes with heels is negligible, however, and does not provide a convincing argument for Oswald's assertion.

The typology is expandable, meaning that anyone using it can compare other English clay pipes to the Port Royal typology and see how they fit (Fox 1999). Other patterns emerged. First, the majority of the pipes fall within the occupation period closest to the earthquake, from 1680 to 1710. Second, the greatest variety of different bowl styles occurred during this period. Why this is the case remains uncertain. Did styles change because of consumer preferences or were they merely at the whim of the pipe maker experimenting with different styles? Another possibility is that the practicalities of overseas shipping could necessitate certain shapes and styles for packing efficiency. Some shapes may have lent themselves better to the overseas haul than others when packed and stored in the holds of ships, as clay pipes were packed in boxes and barrels. The evidence for this comes from the Port Royal probate inventories and archaeological evidence from Port Royal and other submerged sites, such as the 1656 shipwreck of the *Vergulde Draeck* off the coast of western Australia (Green 1977: 152) and the Monte Cristi shipwreck off the northwestern coast of the Dominican Republic (Hall 1996: 152). Archaeologists will be challenged to isolate the reasons for the popularity of certain bowl styles, especially those based on consumer choice and demand, until further research on comparative collections is undertaken. As Noël Hume (1969: 304) maintains, there is still much to be learned about the development of clay tobacco pipes, even more than forty years after his published typology.

But one trend is certain. Most clay tobacco pipes of the seventeenth century had few decorative elements, which is consistent with the Port Royal pipe collection. Some pipes had rouletting, which is done by making small incisions around the bowl rim while the clay is still wet. A few other pipes had diamond and dot patterns on the stem, with the occasional Tudor rose, sometimes indicated by three to seven raised dots. Two such pipes were found at Port Royal, and both were probably Dutch. More elaborate attempts at decoration were made only in the eighteenth century. Decorative pipe stems first appeared in the early eighteenth century, but bowls were also decorated by mid-century (Oswald 1975: 97). Molded decorated pipes had reached their zenith by the nineteenth century; many shared a marked resemblance, suggesting that pipe makers had pattern books available for customers (Oswald 1975: 110).

Analysis of the clay tobacco pipes from Port Royal indicates that 18,537 pipes from the assemblage are clearly English in origin and fall within the occupation period from 1680 to 1710, before and after the devastating earthquake of 1692. A few pipes date to the early founding of Port Royal in 1655, but they make up only a miniscule part of the total assemblage. Makers' marks on some pipes also reinforce their English origins: most were manufactured in Bristol by pipe makers like Llewellin Evans ("LE" pipes), whose pipes were produced for the overseas market. Evans apprenticed a number of other pipe makers, whose products have also been found at Port Royal. Of the thirty-nine makers' marks found at the site, most are "LE" (1,941 pipes). These pipes are evenly distributed, with the greatest concentrations found in Room 5 of Building 1 and Yards 4A/B of Building 4/5. Other "LE" pipes have been found at Nominy Plantation in Virginia, where they represent the bulk of marked pipes (Mitchell 1983: 19). Such pipes also have been found at the St. John's Site at St. Mary's City in Maryland (Hurry and Keeler 1991: 37), at Green Spring Plantation, Virginia (Crass 1988), and in New Brunswick, Canada, as well as at colonial sites along the Eastern Seaboard (Walker 1977: 657–58).

In sum, the assemblage of white clay tobacco pipes from Port Royal is striking in its diversity of pipe bowl styles that cover almost three centuries, thus chronicling advances in clay pipe design and technology. The Port Royal assemblage confirms the growing historical trend toward greater stylistic changes between 1680 and 1710, as well as increasing sophisticated and complicated decorative motifs. This suggests a preference for more elaborate pipes, reflecting the desire for greater diversity in commercially made products in the nineteenth century. The decorative pipes like the Scottish Thistle and Turk's Head pipes found at Port Royal also reveal the high level of moldmaking and mass production achieved since the seventeenth century. Still, the remarkable numbers of seventeenth-century pipes found at Port Royal and other colonial sites bear witness to the ability to mass-produce clay pipes as early as the 1660s, making clay tobacco pipes one of the first truly disposable commodities in the early modern world.

The Documentary Evidence

Although the scientific analyses of clay pipe bowl residues and pollen are fascinating forays into the more science-based side of tobacco and smoking, the mass quantities of pipes speak volumes about the chemical effects of smoking tobacco: it was stimulating, and people liked it. The archaeological evidence of the thousands of clay pipes at Port Royal is borne out by the documentary evidence in the form of the Jamaica Probate Inventories, housed in the Spanish Town archives, and the Bristol Port Records archived in the

Public Records Office in London. Both sources record copious amounts of clay tobacco pipes at Port Royal.

The Port Record shipments of pipes to Jamaica as well as to the other Caribbean and North American colonies numbered in the thousands. The Bristol Port Records for 1682 reveal eighteen shipments from Bristol to Jamaica that included 58,320 pipes (Office of the Exchequer 1682). The Bristol shipments recorded for 1684–1685 jumped to 544,032 pipes (Office of the Exchequer 1694–1695). Comparisons were made to other British North American and Caribbean colonies as part of the triangular trade. For instance, 420,624 pipes were exported to the North American colonies in forty-nine shipments in 1682. In 1694–1695, similarly, 417,816 pipes were sent in forty-eight shipments. Shipments to the Caribbean colonies of Barbados Nevis, Antigua, and St. Lucia tallied 640,080 pipes in 1682 and 601,344 pipes in eighty shipments in 1694–1695, which only slightly exceeds the number of pipes exported to Jamaica alone in 1694–1695. Such large shipments explain why clay tobacco pipes are so plentiful in the archaeological record at Port Royal.

The Jamaica Probate Inventories for 1679–1686 and 1686–1694 are also informative. Essentially lists of a deceased individual's property at the time of death, probate inventories are immensely useful to historical archaeologists and can be used to trace the relationship of status, wealth, and the acquisition of goods (Pendery 1992). This is certainly the case for Port Royal's merchants and ship captains in terms of their tobacco-related inventories.

In examining probate inventories for forty-three Port Royal residents, mostly ship captains and merchants, the inventories of clay pipes are just as breathtaking in terms of sheer quantities. For example, the probate inventory of Port Royal merchant Michael Baker, happily for his widow, totaled 11,520 pipes. Captain Nicholas Verbraack's assets were even more ample at 37,224 clay pipes, while Port Royal merchant Joseph Brown's inventory of 22,752 pipes would have reassured any creditor. Lesser amounts were also recorded: the inventory of Thomas Evans, while not substantial, was still impressive at 432 pipes. We will never know whether these were for retail sale or personal use.

Tobacco-related smoking paraphernalia were also recorded in the probate inventories. Robert Fourth probably methodically used his pair of tongs to pick up two rolls of tobacco that he had stored in a solid brass box, cutting and preparing the tobacco leaves with his razor and sieve before he lit his pipe. The estate of William Haynes, a Port Royal cooper, revealed that he owned a tobacco knife along with a lovely silver box. Robert White's brass tobacco box may not have been as valuable, but he did possess two burning glasses to light his pipe.

The previously discussed collection of red clay pipes from Port Royal is also worth noting. Although the amounts recovered are significantly smaller, the red clay tobacco pipes offer some intriguing evidence that suggests the complex nature of social relations at the port town. The red clay pipes were produced locally, possibly by a combination of free and enslaved Africans as well as free English and indentured servants (Heidtke 1992: 90). The motifs are European, but the stylized *fleur-de-lis* as well as the inclusion of possible elements from African ceramic-making traditions raise questions about the influences of cultural interactions at Port Royal. Further research on these pipes might prove informative in this regard.

A Changing Economy and a World of Goods: Earn to Spend

The archaeological and archival evidence for tobacco smoking in seventeenth-century Port Royal is well substantiated, but what else can the Port Royal clay pipes reveal about changing behaviors of the seventeenth century? The creation of a world system of trade and colonization introduced new consumer goods that included clay tobacco pipes, tobacco, and stimulant foods. In England and the New World colonies, farmers, craftspeople, construction workers, shopkeepers, and others awakened to a world of greater possibilities, offering new sensations, tastes, and acquisitions. As Jan De Vries (2008: 5) claims, it is time to recognize and "celebrate the triumph of the will of the self-fashioning individual" in consumer scholarship.

The exposure to non-necessities such as tobacco, coffee, tea, and chocolate served as a revelation in the seventeenth century, as luxuries offered the pleasurable sensations of taste and their aftereffects. Mintz (1985, 1996: 18) suggests that the desire for and acquisition of such goods represent the first mass consumption of imported foodstuffs among laborers. Small luxury commodities also included objects of personal adornment and decorative household items. Like Port Royal, cities like London and Bristol witnessed the influx of consumer goods previously unknown or only available to those who could afford them. A series of factors converged for the first time, making it possible for more everyday folk to make small purchases of luxury goods. What accounts for this change?

The first factor was a fluctuating economy that was further enhanced by slight increases in wages and earnings throughout the period. Although economic fluctuations, at times volatile, occurred throughout the seventeenth century, periods of greater prosperity were accompanied by increased availability of durable and nondurable goods at lower prices, significantly influencing people's consumer choices and spending habits. Some of the factors contributing to shifts in the economic climate included diversification and innovations in London's overseas trade (see chapter 3). Other factors were the expansion and growth of towns and cities, changing demographics, and the creation of household cottage industries (Nash 1999: 95, 97; Smith 2002).

London and Bristol's commercial trade allowed for the importation of luxury goods such as Chinese porcelain, pewter and silver serving ware, silks, spices, wine goblets, furniture, and other commodities. Although most people could not afford such expensive goods, other items like soap, candles, buttons, lace, and ribbons were commodities within reach of the middling classes. Commercial trade dovetailed with the mass migrations of people from rural to urban areas, helping spur the growth of cities and towns in what historian Peter Borsay (1989: viii; Fox 2004: 90) refers to as an "urban Renaissance." These developments included the proliferation of shops both at Port Royal and in England, which played a critical role in exposing consumers to greater choices in goods. Besides the emporiums that catered to the wealthy, some of the more prosaic types of shops included grocers, apothecaries, and tobacconists (Shammas 1990: 227–28). In fact, the profusion of tobacco retailers spurred anti-tobacconist Barnaby Rich ([1615] 1937: 537) to complain that tobacco was sold in "every Taverne, Inne, and Alehouse."

Grocery items such as pepper, sweets, coffee, and tea were consumed by all social classes. Research by Jeremy Boulton (1996: 269, 272) suggests that wage earners, particularly those in London's construction trade such as bricklayers and carpenters, made a decent living in the capital city, while married women earned wages as domestics and in retail work. Workers had little time to prepare their own food. With some pocket change, they were more dependent on the market for what Mintz (1985: 165) refers to as their "bread

and beer." Martha Carlin (2008) observes that public dining by wage earners began as early as the medieval and Tudor periods. Public eateries were
well established by the seventeenth century, allowing urban populations in
Boston, Bridgetown, or London to rub shoulders with strangers from all
walks of life. Contemporary accounts confirm these developments. London
tradespeople spent "most of their money . . . every Week in the Neighborhood in Strong-Drink, several sorts of Flesh, Bread, Butter, Cheese, Sugar,
Spice, Spanish Fruit and in Cloathing, which caused a quick Circulation in
all Business" (Tryon 1699: 17).

    Another important factor was the growth of cottage industries in pri-
vate homes. Much like budding entrepreneurs who sell goods on eBay to
supplement their household incomes, some families in the seventeenth
century set up small-scale industries in their homes to produce consumables, thus allowing them to enjoy luxuries from the sale of their products.
British manufacturing included the larger industries of textiles, brickmak-
ing, and glassmaking in the formal markets, whereas this less formal market consisted of smaller family enterprises. A study of seventeenth-century
households in northern England suggests that families took on extra work to
maximize their incomes (Fox 2004: 89; Woodward 1994: 25). An important
study of seventeenth-century household and family structures by economic
historian Jan De Vries (2008) also confirms such motivations and activities.
Items made in private homes included buttons and pins as well as lace, soap,
candles, linen, ale, and clocks (Arnold 1977: 314; Fox 2004: 91; Patten 1978:
149; Thirsk 1978: 6). Included among these household industries was the
production of clay tobacco pipes, which proved "more dirty than laborious,
and but moderately profitable" (Campbell 1747: 326). The disposable nature
of tobacco pipes assured a steady livelihood for those who made them, providing a plentiful and accessible supply of both tobacco and pipes for those
who smoked them.

    As all of these factors converged, two phenomena resulted: (1) the emer-
gence of a "consumer revolution"; and (2) "civilizing processes" that took
place in the public sphere. Here lies the crux of significant socioeconomic
changes of the seventeenth century. In terms of a consumer revolution, long
before the advent of the Industrial Revolution, the availability and affordability of nonessential goods became possible, resulting in the development
of new spending habits, consumer choice options, and the acquisition of

luxury goods like ceramics and stimulant foods. The archaeological and archival records confirm these developments with the many thousands of artifacts recovered not only at Port Royal but also throughout colonial sites in
North America and the Caribbean, further supported in recent scholarship
by Carole Shammas (1990, 2000), Lorna Weatherill (1988), Jan De Vries
(2008), Brian Cowan (2011), Fox (2004), and others. The occurrence of a
preindustrial consumerism is no longer a "maybe." It happened, perhaps not
on a scale of the Industrial Revolution but on a scale that signals a definite
change in social behavior for the early modern period. Again, tobacco and
smoking were integral to these developments, owing both to the popularity
of smoking as a pastime and to the clay tobacco pipe's service as one of the
first disposable commodities to hit the ground, literally and figuratively.

With Smoke Comes Drink

Another key development, the "civilizing process" of the public sphere, was
exemplified in the taverns and coffeehouses of London, Port Royal, and the
North American colonies, where tobacco and smoking played an important
role in a small revolution that took place.

Smoking normally requires only one hand, leaving the other free to hold
a drink. The pure and unadulterated joy of smoking tobacco was accentu-
ated by both mild and strong intoxicants as well as by coffee. From Port
Royal to Boston to London, people had no shortage of choices for imbib-
ing. The type of beverage and location in which it was consumed depended
on what patrons could afford, ranging from sipping a fine Madeira in an
upscale tavern to a quick slug of grog (watered-down rum) for the more
rough-and-tumble set. The places for consumers to enjoy tobacco and bev-
erages abounded, including coffeehouses, which became an important institution in seventeenth-century Europe. Unlike tobacco, the importation of
coffee by overseas merchants did not guarantee its success. Historian Brian
Cowan (2011: 15) suggests that coffee only became appealing when it was
"adapted to the various wants and needs of diverse constituencies in the British marketplace."

Although the transformation of English life from the private to public
sphere began in postmedieval London, it was only during the 1600s that
public institutions gained greater importance for socialization. The prec-

edents for Port Royal's plentitude of drinking establishments can be found in the late sixteenth century, when over 17,000 drinking establishments in thirty English counties were recorded, most of which were alehouses (Clark 1983: 2, 14). In 1628 Londoner Richard Rawlidge complained about the proliferation of alehouses, for "every street [is] replenished with them" (Clark 1983: 39). By mid-century England had over 50,000 alehouses, one for every one hundred inhabitants (Reay 1985: 15). Port Royal could also boast its fair share of assorted drinking establishments, prompting one visitor to observe that "there is now resident upon this place ten men to every house that selleth strong liquors" (Burns 1954: 329). During his visit to Port Royal, Ned Ward (1933: 16) bitterly complained about how people took "pleasure in drinking" to the point of shameless debauchery and offensive behavior that made Port Royal the "very Sodom of the Universe."

Little Pipes, Big Transformations

Taken together, the lubricating effects of alcohol and a nicotine-induced state combined to create a pleasurable pastime, complete with its own social rituals and material culture. In a typical scenario, a man or woman would stroll down the streets of Port Royal, Boston, or London, clay tobacco pipe in hand, shortly after purchasing it from a shopkeeper or local pipe maker. This citizen would enter a tavern for lunch, open a pouch, and remove fresh American-grown tobacco leaves that had been processed in England and then re-exported back to the colonies. The smoker would calmly pack a pipe, light it, and deeply inhale, filling the room with the sweet aroma of tobacco.

This scene raises the question of how tobacco was lit throughout the seventeenth and eighteenth centuries. The literature is comparatively silent on this matter, in contrast to the iconography. For example, in the print *The Suckling Faction* (1641), two men are shown enjoying a smoke in a tavern, where one of them is using a nearby candle to light his pipe. Several Dutch paintings, including *Smokers in an Interior* and *A Man and Woman Smoking a Pipe Seated in an Interior with Peasants Playing Cards on a Table* by David Teniers and *A Woman Seated Smoking a Pipe* by Gabriel Metsu, offer one very discernible clue. All three paintings depict a small three-legged ceramic bowl or brazier resting on a table that contains hot coals for lighting a pipe, part of the pipe smoker's equipment. Metsu's painting shows a woman lighting her pipe from the bowl (figure 11; Noël Hume 1982: 95). Tavern and household hearths also provided a steady supply of fire to light a pipe. These were probably the most common methods used until the invention of friction matches in the mid-nineteenth century.

Idling hours away in a tavern, surrounded by smoke and drink, constituted a key pastime for many, particularly for those escaping the hot Caribbean sun of Port Royal. In that respect, smoking provided "compelling satisfactions of a purely psychological nature," such as "the oral satisfaction of clutching a pipe . . . sucking and chewing the stem, and using the mouth in the act of ingestion" (Rublowsky 1974: 76–77). Further satisfaction was derived from the deliberate "action of the fingers and hands in lighting and smoking the pipe" (Rublowsky 1974: 77).

Herein lies one possible explanation for the mass appeal of smoking and intoxicants in the seventeenth century: the ritualization of the actions of lighting and ingestion. Smoking, in a Durkheimian sense, was a small, sacred act in the ordinariness of everyday life. In *Cigarettes Are Sublime* (1993), Richard Klein captures the very essence of this idea. Although his work concerns modern-day cigarette smoking, it is very likely that pipe smoking in the 1600s and 1700s provoked a similar response. The pipe, like the cigarette, in many ways served as a symbolic instrument, acquiring the qualities of a sacred object "endowed with magical properties and seductive charms, surrounded by taboos and an air of danger" (Klein 1993: xii–xiii). Even though pipe smoking was popular, it was not accepted by everyone, so it still retained an aura of forbidden pleasure, especially for women.

In his examination of social change as it relates to the increased use of intoxicants, Phil Withington (2011) observes that tea, coffee, and sugar, along with the rise in tobacco smoking and the increased production of distilled alcohol products, all emerged at a similar time in the seventeenth century. Accompanying the proliferation of these new consumer products were the household money-making activities to support consumer spending on these foodstuffs.

In this changing social realm, the acts of drinking and smoking soon became associated with a kind of sophistication. The politics of taste surrounding consumption were acted out in the public sphere, mainly in the company of men, who jockeyed for prestige and status amid quick humor and merrymaking (Withington 2011: 632). In a sense, men were forming their own fictive kinship, a club or brotherhood of smokers and drinkers who had their own rituals that "were normative and stylized aspects to their social identity," particularly among well educated men who frequented the more upscale taverns and coffeehouses (Withington 2011: 632). Smoking tobacco, along with drinking, thus served an important binding agent for everyday sociability.

Philosopher Jürgen Habermas (1989: 25, 30–36) maintains that the transformation of English culture in the seventeenth century developed in the public sphere, where people came "together to form a public, readied themselves to compel public authority to legitimate itself before public opinion" (Habermas 1989: 25). The public forum was embodied in institutions such as coffeehouses and public houses, including taverns, alehouses, and clubs, where conversation functioned as a kind of moral instruction for shaping attitudes and manners (Fox 2004: 92; Habermas 1989: 30–36). Historian Beat Kümin (2007: 4) states that public houses were the "most prominent communication spaces in early modern localities." In fact, public houses can be interpreted as microcosms of early modern society as well as "micro-laboratories for the study of interactions between individuals and groups with distinct agendas" (Kümin 2007: 4).

The many taverns and other drinking establishments in England and Port Royal attest to this social development. It fits well with the urbanization of the early modern era that saw a rise in the numbers of shops and public establishments related to eating and drinking.

In this context, smoking and drinking as shared pastimes encouraged conviviality through conversation and promoted friendly relations. An entry in Richard Lowe's diary illustrates this point: Lowe ([1663–1674] 1938: 43–44) brings his Lancashire neighbor "a pipe of tobacco" as a gesture of friendship. In this same spirit, Peter Pope (2004: 396) refers to alcohol and clay tobacco pipes as "little hearths" where "each satisfied the need for warmth," but not in the actual physical sense. Rather, tobacco is something to be shared and offers social warmth, a way to create sociability among the cod fishermen and settlers of Ferryland colony in seventeenth-century Newfoundland (Pope 2004: 397).

The sociability of smoking can also be demonstrated through such useful sources as Dutch genre paintings, which offer iconographic evidence in depictions of smoking and drinking in public settings based on real-life observations. Depictions of drunks passed out after a long night of revelry, broken clay pipes strewn on the floor, and disrupted game boards make up some of the vivid images of tavern life, along with scenes of large gatherings of men, women, and children seated around a table, plied with food and drink. The sensuousness of the acts of drinking, smoking, and eating are not lost on the viewer; in fact, the contentment portrayed is not only palpable but almost enviable.

Conclusion

What can we learn from a body of data like the Port Royal clay pipes, and how can they be useful in interpreting social change in the early modern era? Looking back on English history, the early seventeenth century was a period of emergence from a repressive European feudal system, where masses of rural refugees left for the growing towns and cities of England and overseas colonies like Port Royal, tasting true freedom for the first time in their lives.

Smoking tobacco and socializing in public settings presented a novel experience for members of a society experiencing transition. Alcohol as a social lubricant helped to ease anxieties in a changing landscape of new ideas, places, and social mores in a society undergoing profound cultural change (Smith 2008: 99). The same could be said for tobacco. As Mintz (1985: 99–100) reminds us, the arrival of tobacco and other drug foods signaled the introduction of "tea time," along with other social institutions that offered the opportunity to experience new sensations and stimuli, often in a public setting that encouraged the development of "civilized" behavior and the sharing of ideas.

The appearance of tobacco and alcohol as well as sugar, coffee, tea, and chocolate ushered in an era of new dietary stimulants previously unavailable to most people. The growth of cities and the proliferation of shops, taverns, and coffeehouses provided the opportunity to socialize and exercise consumer choice where none had existed before. The chance for people to generate some extra revenue to supplement household incomes in a time of fluctuating prices (sometimes in favor of the consumer) offered the opportunity for many people to make small purchases, heralding the advent of a preindustrial consumerism that reflected changing tastes, new social habits, and options.

In sum, as an assemblage of artifacts, the Port Royal pipes cannot fully illuminate the lives of the people who smoked them. But they can provide the archaeological evidence for social change at a time when the old order was about to experience a dramatic and fundamental shift. As part of seventeenth-century material culture, the clay pipes reflect the more ephemeral moments in the life of a smoker—the pleasurable, social, and symbolic aspects in the small act of lighting and smoking a pipe. For the archaeologist, clay tobacco pipes also offer a window into seventeenth-century daily life and customs within the cultural context of a New World colony in the throes of change. The pipes allow the archaeologist to take a glimpse of an earlier time from a distance: a society emerging from a feudal past to a future rich with possibilities.

7

Conclusion

As Frederick Smith (2008: 134) reminds us in *The Archaeology of Alcohol and Drinking*, commodity-based research can have far-reaching implications in the study of the early modern era. Like sugar and alcohol, tobacco had its place in the American experience, often accompanying alcohol in social settings. The distinct aspects of tobacco and smoking unique to the Americas and the American experience can be summarized in a few ways. First and foremost, tobacco was indigenous to the Americas, already growing before the first explorer sailed to New World. The "discovery" of tobacco may be attributed to the Europeans, but its place in ritualized practices and traditions long preceded the arrival of the first barque to American shores. Indigenous peoples throughout the Americas had been smoking and ingesting tobacco in a variety of forms, from the rolled "cigars" of Caribbean Amerindians to the stone pipes of the early mound-builders of the central and southern portions of North America.

The colonization of the Caribbean region as the gateway to the Americas was essentially built on two agricultural commodities: tobacco and sugar. The mass production of tobacco is essentially an American phenomenon, because it was the first true commercially grown product in the Caribbean and Chesapeake regions. Colonial agronomy began with tobacco farmers. As they grew and tested different varieties, their success contributed to the early foundations of capitalism through a world system of colonial investments and complex trade networks involving the exchange of raw materials and manufactured goods. The establishment of trade and colonization through agricultural commodities eventually propelled Great Britain to empire and hegemonic power.

None of this would have been possible without the importation of en-slaved Africans, whose hard labor made it possible to plant, care for, and harvest tobacco for the growing coffers of the European powers intent on establishing tobacco plantations throughout the Caribbean, with the Chesa-peake tobacco growers taking the lead. As economic historians have demon-strated, tobacco was the first remunerative crop in the Americas, paving the way for the sugar plantocratic regimes.

As tobacco became an integral part of American life, over a 300-year period it came to represent a symbol of identity, from the wealthy planter class to immigrant laborers. What makes tobacco and smoking unique to the American experience is the way in which this weed played a role in almost every major shift in American life, from rural farmstead communities to the frenzied pace of a burgeoning industrialized and urban America. Smoking tobacco was the salve that made these transitions easier; it was a binder of human experience regardless of gender, class, or ethnicity. Most people smoked until recently, to assuage fear and anxiety, stare down boredom, re-lax, or assert notions of individuality and identity. Only in America could the Marlboro Man exist: a rugged individual, figment of the collective imagina-tion or real enough to pursue life, liberty, and democratic freedoms by choice. It has been proposed by some scholars that the radical ideas of the Ameri-can Revolution were formed in the taverns of the American colonies, surely fueled and fanned by the whiff of the clay tobacco pipe and "stronge drink."

In essence, tobacco and smoking have come to signify creativity and rebel-lion in the American experience, as continually demonstrated throughout American history. Where would Marlon Brando and James Dean be without the image of the rebel smoker? Women were perceived as feminists if they smoked a certain brand, because they had come a long way with the vote, contraception, and smoking in public. The rest of the world caught on, copy-ing these images and adapting them to fit their own cultural and national heroes, but this story originated on American shores.

It is not merely modern advertising, the arts, and popular media that broadcast public sentiments about tobacco and smoking. Its acceptance is well documented in the archaeological record, demonstrating a long history of smoking and tobacco use. If continued tobacco consumption were merely a matter of addiction, this might easily explain away the popularity of smoking and certain social behaviors. But the ample literature on the social history of smoking, the rich documentary evidence, and the extensive archaeological record reveal a nuanced and detailed tapestry of tobacco usage and smoking. From this perspective, historical archaeology has much to offer in understanding human expression and past behaviors in the consumption of tobacco and its deeper symbolic meanings. Whether as a trade item between European and Euroamerican fur traders and Native Americans, as a form of Irish identity in urban America, or as a soothing companion to a homesick soldier on the Western frontier, tobacco has retained a strong presence throughout the American experience.

It has been shown that tobacco played a critical role in the developing Atlantic world of colonization and trade as a desired commodity, contributing to an early preindustrial consumerism in the foundational development of capitalist economies. In their compelling study, Jankowiak and Bradburd (1996:720) observe that in a burgeoning capitalist world system, a pattern emerged whereby colonial actors used stimulants to induce native peoples to perform laborious tasks by fostering chemical dependencies. In their case studies, alchohol played that role; however, a similar case could be made for tobacco. Additionally, tobacco and smoking have functioned as a safety valve, calming the nerves and encouraging sociability and manners in the public sphere. Tobacco has also provided a means of negotiating difficult relations between Native Americans and colonizers or traders, often fraught with the potential for violence.

Tobacco and smoking have served to express a wide range of sentiments and needs among human populations. Tobacco has reinforced notions of individuality, patriotism, class, gender, and ethnic identity, regardless of the possible outcomes, including stained and worn teeth, addiction, or lung cancer. Despite meeting disapproval in some segments of society, smoking still acts as a vehicle for rebellion and resistance, allowing for personal and group identities. A recent article in the *New York Times* (Fernandez 2011) highlights a retired police officer's personal defiance of current politics and tax laws. In her Brooklyn backyard, she has opted to grow, process, and smoke her own tax-free cigarettes. Teenagers in their first taste of "freedom" may sneak a cigarette to assert their independence from their parents and reinforce their peer-recognized identities. In fact, tobacco is never far from controversy; even in the current scientific debate over genetically modified foods, tobacco was the first genetically engineered plant to be subject to experimentation (Bevan et al. 1983, cited in Lemaux 2008: 777).

Although images of the carefree smoker are long gone from the billboards of North America, the association of smoking with individuality in a cult of defiance is valued in American society, as proved by robust cigarette sales. Four hundred years after the introduction of tobacco, its production, consumption, and distribution are worldwide and still going strong, as tobacco and smoking continue to be highly relevant throughout the globe. For example, tobacco and cigarettes serve as a marker of status and class in China, as business leaders compete with one another through the brands they smoke. As journalist Peter Hessler (2011: 233) observed, "Most [Chinese] men don't worry that cigarettes are bad for their health. In the southern city of Wenzhou, I once met a businessman in his thirties who described smoking as a career move. When I asked him if he wanted to quit, the man looked at me like I was crazy. 'No way!' he said. 'I know it's not good for you, but I'm young so I don't feel any effect. And it's important for business. If you're trying to pull *guanxi* with somebody, you have to take him out to dinner, and you need to smoke and drink with him.'" From an anthropological perspective, recent developments in the material culture of tobacco and smoking are fascinating—from plastic BIC butane lighters to a recent surge in electronic cigarettes—only reinforcing the enduring popularity of smoking. What will archaeologists expect to find 400 years from now? They can look forward to the material evidence of an enduring cultural practice.

In the long-term study of foodstuffs and stimulants that societies have appropriated throughout time and across space, tobacco has been and continues to be integral to humankind. As historical archaeologists recover clay tobacco pipes and other tobacco-related artifacts, the challenges to garner meaning from this body of material culture are ongoing. Tobacco-related research holds great promise in furthering our understanding of culture change and cultural adaptation to an ever-changing world over the last 300 years, whether in the crowded taverns of seventeenth-century Port Royal, Jamaica, or in the lively saloons of the American West. The remnants of a tobacco-loving society have left tantalizing clues to their past, which has yet to bare all of its secrets.

References Cited

Abel, Thomas. 2007. "World-Systems as Complex Human Ecosystems." In *The World System and the Earth System*, edited by A. Hornborg and C. Crumley, 56–73. Walnut Creek, Calif.: Left Coast Press.

Adams, William Y., and Ernest W. Adams. 2007. *Archaeological Typology and Practical Reality: A Dialectical Approach to Artifact Classification and Sorting*. Cambridge: Cambridge University Press.

Agbe-Davies, Anna S. 2004. "The Production and Consumption of Smoking Pipes along the Tobacco Coast." In *Smoking and Culture: The Archaeology of Tobacco Pipes in Eastern North America*, edited by S. Rafferty and R. Mann, 273–304. Knoxville: University of Tennessee Press.

Akers, Donna. 1999. "Removing the Heart of the Choctaw People: Indian Removal from a Native Perspective." *American Indian Culture and Research Journal* 23(3): 63–76.

Alexander, Anna, and Mark S. Roberts. 2003. "Introduction." In *High Culture: Reflections on Addiction and Modernity*, edited by A. Alexander and M. S. Roberts, 1–15. Albany: State University of New York Press.

Alsop, George. 1638. *A Character of the Province of Maryland*. Early Americas Digital Archive.

Alt, Kurt W., and Sandra L. Pichler. 2003. "Artificial Modifications of Human Teeth." In *Dental Anthropology: Fundamentals, Limits and Prospects*, edited by K. W. Alt, F. W. Rösing, and M. Teschler-Nicola, 387–415. New York: Springer.

Alvey, R. C., R. R. Laxton, and G. F. Paechter. 1979. "Statistical Analysis of Some Nottingham Clay Tobacco Pipes." In *The Archaeology of the Clay Tobacco Pipe— Britain: The Midlands and Eastern England*, Vol. 1, edited by P. Davey, 229–53. BAR British Series 63. Oxford: British Archaeological Reports.

Apperson, George L. 1916. *The Social History of Smoking*. New York: G. P. Putnam's Sons.

Armstrong, Douglas V. 1990. *The Old Village and Great House: An Archaeological and Historical Examination of Drax Hall Plantation, St. Ann's Bay, Jamaica*. Champaign: University of Illinois Press.

Arnold, C. J. 1977. "The Tobacco Pipe Industry: An Economic Study." In *Pottery and Early Commerce: Characterization and Trade in Roman and Later Ceramics*, edited by D. P. S. Peacock, 313–36. London: Academic Press.

Asbury, Herbert. (1928) 2008. *The Gangs of New York: An Informal History of the Underworld*. Reprint. New York: Vintage.

Ayto, Eric G. 2002. *Clay Tobacco Pipes*. Aylesbury, Buckinghamshire: Shire Publications.

Barham, Henry. 1722. *The Civil History of Jamaica to the Year 1722*. Sloane Manuscript 12422. British Museum Library, London.

Barnard, Etwell A. B. 1948. *A Seventeenth-Century Country Gentleman (Sir Francis Throckmorton, 1640–80)*. Cambridge: W. Heffer and Sons.

Barrett, James R. 2012. *The Irish Way: Becoming American in the Multiethnic City*. New York: Penguin Books.

Beaud, Michel. 1983. *A History of Capitalism 1500–1980*. Translated by T. Dickerman and A. Lefebvre. New York: Monthly Review Press.

Beaudry, Mary C., Lauren J. Cook, and Stephen A. Mrozowski. 1991. "Artifacts and Active Voices: Material Culture as Social Discourse." In *The Archaeology of Inequality*, edited by R. H. McGuire and R. Paynter, 150–91. Oxford: Basil Blackwell.

Beer, George L. 1948. *The Commercial Policy of England*. New York: Peter Smith.

———. (1908) 1959. *The Origins of the British Colonial System 1578–1660*. Gloucester: Peter Smith.

Bell, Alison. 2005. "White Ethnogenesis and Gradual Capitalism: Perspectives from Colonial Archaeological Sites in the Chesapeake." *American Anthropologist* 107(3): 446–60.

Berg, O. C. and C. F. Schmidt. 1858–1863. *Darstellung und Beschreibung sämmtlicher in der Pharmacopoea Borussica aufgeführten offizinellen Gewächse, etc.* Vol. 2. Leipzig: Arthur Felix.

Bevan, M. W., R. B. Flavell, and M. D. Chilton. 1983. "A Chimeric Antibiotic Resistance Gene as a Selectable Marker for Plant Cell Transformation." *Nature* 304: 184–87.

Binford, Lewis. 1962. "A New Method of Calculating Dates from Kaolin Pipe Stem Samples." *Southeastern Archaeological Conference Newsletter* 9: 19–21.

Blakeslee, Donald J. 1981. "The Origin and Spread of the Calumet Ceremony." *American Antiquity* 46(4): 759–68.

Borsay, Peter. 1989. *The English Urban Renaissance: Culture and Society in the Provincial Town 1660–1770*. Oxford: Clarendon Press.

Boulton, Jeremy. 1996. "Wage Labour in Seventeenth-Century London." *Economic History Review* 50(2): 268–90.

Bourdieu, Pierre. 1984. *Distinction: A Social Critique of the Judgment of Taste*. Translated by R. Nice. Cambridge, Mass.: Harvard University Press.

Bradburn, Douglas M., and John C. Coombs. 2006. "Smoke and Mirrors: Reinterpreting the Society and Economy of the Seventeenth-Century Chesapeake." *Atlantic Studies* 3(2): 131–57.

Bradley, Charles S. 2000. "Smoking Pipes for the Archaeologist." In *Studies in Material Culture Research*, edited by K. Karkins, 104–33. California, Pa.: Society for Historical Archaeology.

Braithwait, Richard. 1617. *The Smoaking Age: Or, The Life and Death of Tobacco*. London. The George Arents Collection, New York Public Library, New York.

Braudel, Fernand. 1973. *Capitalism and Material Life, 1400–1800*. Translated by M. Kochan. New York: Harper and Row.

———. 1977. *Afterthoughts on Material Civilization and Capitalism*. Translated by P. M. Ranum. Baltimore: Johns Hopkins University Press.

———. 1979. *The Structures of Everyday Life: The Limits of the Possible*. Vol. 1. New York: Harper and Row.

Breen, T. H. 1985. *Tobacco Culture: The Mentality of the Great Tidewater Planters on the Eve of Revolution*. Princeton: Princeton University Press.

Brighton, Stephen A. 2009. *Historical Archaeology of the Irish Diaspora: A Transnational Approach*. Knoxville: University of Tennessee Press.

Brodie, Janet Farrell, and Marc Redfield. 2002. "Introduction." In *High Anxieties: Cultural Studies in Addiction*, edited by J. F. Brodie and M. Redfield, 1–15. Berkeley: University of California Press.

Brongers, George A. 1964. *Nicotiana Tabacum: The History of Tobacco and Tobacco Smoking in the Netherlands*. Amsterdam: H.J.W. Becht's Uitgeversmaatschappij.

Brooks, Jerome E. 1937. *Tobacco: Its History, Illustrated by the Books, Manuscripts and Engravings in the Library of George Arents, Jr.* 4 vols. New York: Rosenback Company.

Brown, Ian W. 1989. "The Calumet Ceremony in the Southeast and Its Archaeological Manifestations." *American Antiquity* 54(2): 311–31.

Bryant, Vaughn, Sarah Kampbell, and Jerome Hall. 2012. "Tobacco Pollen: Archaeological and Forensic Applications." *Palynology* 36(2): 208–23.

Burns, Alan C. 1954. *History of the British West Indies*. London: George Allen and Unwin.

Callage, Rosemarie, John Kille, and Al Luckenbach. 1999. "An Analysis of 17th Century Clay Tobacco Pipes from the Chaney's Hills Site (18AN1084)." *Maryland Archaeology* 35(2): 27–33.

Campbell, R. 1747. *The London Tradesman*. Microfilm. Sterling Evans Library, Texas A&M University, College Station.

Cande, Kathleen H. 2000. "Ritual and Material Culture as Keys to Cultural Continuity: Native American Interaction with Europeans in Eastern Arkansas, 1541–1682." In *Interpretations of Native North American Life*, edited by M. S. Nassaney and E. S. Johnson, 32–52. Gainesville: University Press of Florida.

Cantwell, Anne-Marie, and Diana diZerega Wall. 2001. *Unearthing Gotham: The Archaeology of New York City*. New Haven: Yale University Press.

Capone, Patricia, and Elinor Downs. 2004. "Red Clay Tobacco Pipes: A Petrographic Window into Seventeenth-Century Economics at Jamestown, Virginia and New England." In *Smoking and Culture: The Archaeology of Tobacco Pipes in Eastern North America*, edited by S. Rafferty and R. Mann, 305–16. Knoxville: University of Tennessee Press.

Carlin, Martha. 2008. "'What Say You to a Piece of Beef and Mustard?': The Evolution of Public Dining in Medieval and Tudor England." *Huntington Library Quarterly* 71(1): 199–217.

Chase-Dunn, Christopher, and Thomas D. Hall. 1997. *Rise and Demise: Comparing World-Systems*. Boulder: Westview Press.

Claney, Jane Perkins. 2004. *Rockingham Ware in American Culture, 1830–1930: Reading Historical Artifacts*. Lebanon, N.H.: University Press of New England.

Clark, Peter. 1983. *The English Alehouse: A Social History 1200–1830*. London: Longman.

Clarkson, Leslie A. 1972. *The Pre-Industrial Economy in England, 1500–1750*. New York: Schocken Books.

Clemens, Paul G. E. 2011. "Reimagining the Political Economy of Early Virginia." *William and Mary Quarterly* 68(3): 393–97.

Coclanis, Peter. 2011. "New Views of the Early Chesapeake." *William and Mary Quarterly* 68(3): 398–404.

Columbus, Christopher. (1492) 1992. *The Voyage of Christopher Columbus*. Edited and translated by J. Cummins. New York: St. Martin's Press.

Compleat Tradesman. 1684. *The Exact Dealers Daily Companion.* London: John Dunton.

Cook, Lauren J. 1989. "Tobacco-Related Material and the Construction of Working-Class Culture." In *Interdisciplinary Investigations of the Boott Mills, Lowell, Massachusetts, Volume III: The Boarding House System as a Way of Life*, edited by M. C. Beaudry and S. A. Mrozowsi, 209–29. Cultural Resources Management Study No. 21. Boston: Division of Cultural Resources, North Atlantic Regional Office, National Park Service, United States Department of the Interior.

———. 1997. "'Promiscuous Smoking': Interpreting Gender and Tobacco Use in the Archaeological Record." *Northeast Historical Archaeology* 26: 23–38.

Coombs, John C. 2011. "The Phases of Conversion: A New Chronology for the Rise of Slavery in Early Virginia." *William and Mary Quarterly* 68(3): 332–60.

Corti, Egon Caesar, Count. 1932. *A History of Smoking.* New York: Harcourt, Brace.

Cotter, John L. 1994. *Archaeological Investigations at Jamestown, Virginia.* Archaeological Society of Virginia, Special Publication No. 32. Washington, D.C.: National Park Service, United States Department of the Interior.

Courtwright, David T. 2002. *Forces of Habit: Drugs and the Making of the Modern World.* Cambridge, Mass.: Harvard University Press.

Cowan, Brian. 2011. *The Social Life of Coffee: The Emergence of the British Coffeehouse.* New Haven: Yale University Press.

Cox, C. Jane, Al Luckenbach, Dave Gadsby, and Shawn Sharpe. 2005. *Locally-Made Tobacco Pipes in the Colonial Chesapeake.* Paper Presented at the 2005 Annual Meeting of the Society for Historical Archaeology in York, England.

Crain, Christopher, Kevin Farmer, Frederick H. Smith, and Karl Watson. 2004. "Human Skeletal Remains from an Unmarked African Burial Ground in the Pierhead Section of Bridgetown, Barbados." *Journal of the Barbados Museum and Historical Society* 50: 66–83.

Crass, David Colin. 1988. "The Clay Pipes from Green Spring Plantation (44JC9), Virginia." *Historical Archaeology* 22(1): 83–97.

Croker, Thomas Crofton. 1835. "Ancient Tobacco Pipes." *Dublin Penny Journal* 4(160): 28–30.

Cronin, William. 1983. *Changes in the Land: Indians, Colonists, and the Ecology of New England.* New York: Hill and Wang.

Crossley, David W. 1990. *Post-Medieval Archaeology in Britain.* London: Leicester University Press.

Dallal, Diane. 2004. "The Tudor Rose and the Fleur-de-lis: Women and Iconography in Seventeenth-Century Dutch Clay Pipes Found in New York City." In *Smoking and Culture: The Archaeology of Tobacco Pipes in Eastern North America,* edited by S. Rafferty and R. Mann, 207–39. Knoxville: University of Tennessee Press.

Daniels, Bruce C. 1993. "Sober Mirth and Pleasant Poisons: Puritan Ambivalence toward Leisure and Recreation in Colonial New England." *American Studies* 34(1): 121–37.

———. 1995. *Puritans at Play: Leisure and Recreation in Colonial New England.* New York: St. Martin's Press.

Davis, Ralph. 1962. "English Foreign Trade, 1700–1774." *Economic History Review* 15(2): 285–303.

Deetz, James. 1977. *In Small Things Forgotten: The Archaeology of Early American Life.* New York: Anchor Books.

———. 1993. *Flowerdew Hundred: The Archaeology of a Virginia Plantation, 1619–1864.* Charlottesville: University Press of Virginia.

De Vries, Jan. 2008. *The Industrious Revolution: Consumer Behavior and the Household Economy, 1650 to the Present*. Cambridge: Cambridge University Press.

Diderot, Denis, and Jean le Rond d'Alembert, eds. 1751–1772. "Art de faire les pipes." In *Encyclopédie, ou Dictionnaire Raisonné des Sciences, des Arts et des Métiers*, vol. 4 and vol. 1, supplement, plate 1 (206). Paris: Royal Academy of Sciences.

Diner, Hasia R. 1996. "'The Most Irish City in the Union': The Era of the Great Migration, 1844–1877." In *The New York Irish*, edited by R. H. Baylor and T. J. Meagher, 87–106. Baltimore: Johns Hopkins Press.

Dixon, Kelly J. 2005. *Boomtown Saloons: Archaeology and History in Virginia City*. Reno: University of Nevada Press.

———. 2006. "Survival of Biological Evidence on Artifacts: Applying Forensic Techniques at the Boston Saloon, Virginia City, Nevada." *Historical Archaeology* 40(3): 20–30.

Dolan, Jay P. 2008. *The Irish Americans: A History*. New York: Bloomsbury Press.

Douglas, Mary, and Baron Isherwood. 1996. *The World of Goods*. New York: Routledge.

Dow, George F. 1988. *Every Day Life in the Massachusetts Bay Colony*. New York: Dover Publications.

Dunn, Richard S. 1973. *Sugar and Slaves: The Rise of the Planter Class in the English West Indies, 1624–1713*. New York: W. W. Norton.

D. W. 1915. "Briar Wood for Pipes." *Bulletin of Miscellaneous Information (Royal Gardens, Kew)* 3: 127–28.

Earle, Carville. 1979. "Environment, Disease, and Mortality in Early Virginia." In *The Chesapeake in the Seventeenth Century: Essays on Anglo-American Society*, edited by T. W. Tate and D. L. Ammerman, 96–125. Chapel Hill: University of North Carolina Press.

Eerkens, Jelmer, Shannon Tushingham, Kari Lentz, Jennifer Blake, Dominique Ardura, Mine Palazoglu, and Oliver Fiehn. 2012. "GC/MS Analysis of Residues Reveals Nicotine in Two Late Prehistoric Pipes from CA-ALA-554." *Society for California Archaeology Proceedings* 26: 212–19.

Eisenmenger, Nina, and Stefan Giljum. 2007. "Evidence from Societal Metabolism Studies for Ecological Unequal Trade." In *The World System and the Earth System*, edited by A. Hornborg and C. Crumley, 288–302. Walnut Creek, Calif.: Left Coast Press.

Emerson, Matthew C. 1999. "African Inspiration in a New World Art and Artifact: Decorated Tobacco Pipes from the Chesapeake." In *"I, Too, Am America": Archaeological Studies of African-American Life*, edited by T. A. Singleton, 47–82. Charlottesville: University Press of Virginia.

Fairholt, Frederick William. 1859. *Tobacco: Its History and Associations: Including an*

Account of the Plant and Its Manufacture; with Its Modes of Use in All Ages and Countries. London: Chapman and Hall.

Felberbaum, Michael. 2011. "Personalized Clay Pipes Unearthed at Jamestown." *Associated Press*, January 1.

Fenton, William N. 1953. *The Iroquois Eagle Dance: An Offshoot of the Calumet Dance*. Bulletin 156. Washington, D.C.: Smithsonian Institution Bureau of American Ethnology.

Fernandez, Manny. 2011. "Now in Brooklyn, Homegrown Tobacco: Local, Rebellious and Tax Free." *New York Times*, February 24.

Field, Edward. 1897. *The Colonial Tavern*. Providence, R.I.: Preston and Rounds.

Fiennes, Celia. 1982. *The Illustrated Journeys of Celia Fiennes, 1685–1712*. Edited by C. Morris. London: Morris MacDonald.

Fisher, Robert Lewis. 1939. *The Odyssey of Tobacco*. Litchfield, Conn.: Prospect Press.

Fowler, William S. 1955. "Chronology of Some Kaolin Pipe Types." *Bulletin of the Massachusetts Archaeology Society* 27: 14–17.

Fox, Georgia L. 1999. *The Kaolin Clay Pipe Tobacco Collection from Port Royal, Jamaica*. The Archaeology of the Clay Tobacco Pipe, vol. 15, edited by P. Davey. BAR International Series 809. Oxford: British Archaeological Reports.

———. 2004. "Little Tubes of Mighty Power: How Clay Tobacco Pipes from Port Royal, Jamaica, Reflect Socioeconomic Change in Seventeenth-Century English Culture and Society." In *Values and Valuables: From the Sacred to the Symbolic*, edited by C. Werner and D. Bell, 79–100. Walnut Creek, Calif.: AltaMira Press.

Fox, Richard A., Melissa A. Connor, and Dick Harmon. 2000. *Archaeological Perspectives on the Battle of the Little Bighorn*. Norman: University of Oklahoma Press.

Frank, André Gunder. 1978. *World Accumulation, 1492–1789*. New York: Monthly Review Press.

Gadsby, David. 2002. "Industrial Re-Use of Domestic Ceramics at Swan Cove (18AN934)." *Maryland Archaeology* 38(1): 19–26.

Galle, Jillian E. 2010. "Costly Signaling and Gendered Social Strategies among Slaves in the Eighteenth-Century Chesapeake: An Archaeological Perspective." *American Antiquity* 75(1): 19–43.

Goodman, Jordan. 1993. *Tobacco in History: The Cultures of Dependence*. New York: Routledge.

Goodwin, Lorinda B. R. 1999. *An Archaeology of Manners: The Polite World of the Merchant Elite of Colonial Massachusetts*. New York: Kluwer Academic.

Gosden, Chris, and Chantal Knowles. 2001. *Collecting Colonialism: Material Culture and Colonial Change*. Oxford: Berg Publishers.

Graham, Willie, Carter L. Hudgins, Carl R. Lounsbury, Fraser D. Neiman, and James P. Whittenburg. 2007. "Archaeological and Architectural Perspectives on the Seventeenth-Century Chesapeake." *William and Mary Quarterly* 64(3): 451–522.

Green, Jeremy N. 1977. *The Loss of the Verenigde Oostindische Compahnie Jacht Verguilde Draeck, Western Australia 1656*. Part 1. BAR Supplementary Series 36. Oxford: British Archaeological Reports.

Groover, Mark D. 2003. *An Archaeological Study of Rural Capitalism and Material Life: The Gibbs Farmstead in Southern Appalachia, 1790–1920*. New York: Kluwer Academic/Plenum Publishers.

———. 2008. *The Archaeology of North American Farmsteads*. Gainesville: University Press of Florida.

Habermas, Jürgen. 1989. *The Structural Transformation of the Public Sphere: An Inquiry into a Category of Bourgeois Society*. Cambridge, Mass.: MIT Press.

Hakluyt, Richard. 1904. *The Principal Voyages, Traffiques and Discoveries of the English Nation*, Vol. 10. Glasgow: James MacLehose and Sons.

Hall, Jerome H. 1996. "A Seventeenth-Century Northern European Merchant Shipwreck in Monte Cristi Bay, Dominican Republic." PhD dissertation, Texas A&M University, College Station.

Hall, Martin, and Stephen W. Silliman. 2006. "Introduction: Archaeology of the Modern World." In *Historical Archaeology*, edited by M. Hall and S. W. Silliman, 1–19. Malden, Mass.: Blackwell Press.

Hall, Robert L. 1977. "An Anthropocentric Perspective for Eastern United States Prehistory." *American Antiquity* 42(4): 499–518.

Hall, Thomas. 2000. "Frontiers, Ethnogenesis, and World Systems: Rethinking the Theories." In *A World-Systems Reader*, edited by T. Hall, 237–70. New York: Rowman and Littlefield.

Hamilton, D. L. 1984. "Preliminary Report on the Archaeological Excavations of the Submerged Remains of Port Royal, Jamaica, 1981–1982." *International Journal of Nautical Archaeology and Underwater Exploration* 13: 11–25.

———. 1985. "The City under the Sea." In *Science Year: The World Book Science Annual*, 92–109. Chicago: World Book.

———. 1986. "Port Royal Revisited." In *Underwater Archaeology: The Proceedings of the Fourteenth Conference on Underwater Archaeology*, edited by C. R. Cummings, 73–81. Special Publication No. 7. San Marino, Calif.: Fathom Eight.

———. 1988. "Underwater Excavations of the 17th-Century Buildings at the Intersection of Lime and Queen Streets." In *Proceedings from the Society for Historical Archaeology Conference, Reno, Nevada, January 1988*, edited by James Delgado, 9–12. Special Publications Series No. 7. Maryland: Society for Historical Archaeology.

———. 1990. "Port Royal 1990: The Last Excavation Season." *Institute of Nautical Archaeology Newsletter* 17(4): 14–17.

————. 1991. "A Decade of Excavations at Port Royal, Jamaica." In *Underwater Archaeology Proceedings from the Society for Historical Archaeology Conference*, edited by J. D. Broadwater, 90–94. Richmond: Society for Historical Archaeology.

————. 1992. "Simon Benning, Pewterer of Port Royal." In *Text-Aided Archaeology*, edited by B. J. Little, 39–53. Boca Raton: CRC Press.

————. 2000. *The Port Royal Project: Archaeological Excavation*. College Station: Texas A&M University. http://nautarch.tamu.edu/portroyal/archhist.htm.

Hamshere, Cyril. 1972. *The British in the Caribbean*. Cambridge, Mass.: Harvard University Press.

Hancock, David. 2000. "A 'Revolution in the Trade': Wine Distribution and the Development of the Infrastructure of the Atlantic Market Economy, 1703–1807." In *The Early Modern Atlantic Economy*, edited by J. J. McCusker and K. Morgan, 105–53. Cambridge: Cambridge University Press.

Handler, Jerome S. 1983. "An African Pipe from a Slave Cemetery in Barbados, West Indies." In *The Archaeology of the Clay Tobacco Pipe, Vol. VIII, America*, edited by P. Davey, 245–54. BAR International Series 175. Oxford: British Archaeological Reports.

————. 2009. "The Middle Passage and the Material Culture of Captive Africans." *Slavery and Abolition* 30(1): 1–26.

Handler, Jerome S., and Frederick W. Lange. 1978. *Plantation Slavery in Barbados: An Archaeological and Historical Investigation*. Cambridge, Mass.: Harvard University Press.

Handler, Jerome S., and Neil Norman. 2007. "From West Africa to Barbados: A Rare Pipe from a Plantation Slave Cemetery." *African Diaspora Archaeology Network Newsletter* 9: 1–12.

Hariot, Thomas. (1590) 1972. *A Briefe and True Report of the New Found Land of Virginia*. New York: Dover Publications.

Harrington, James C. 1954. "Dating Stem Fragments of Seventeenth and Eighteenth Century Clay Tobacco Pipes." *Quarterly Bulletin of the Archaeological Society of Virginia* 9(1): 10–14.

Hatfield, April Lee. 2004. *Atlantic Virginia: Intercolonial Relations in the Seventeenth Century*. Philadelphia: University of Pennsylvania Press.

Hawke, David F. 1988. *Everyday Life in Early America*. New York: Harper and Row.

Heath, Barbara J. 1999. *Hidden Lives: The Archaeology of Slave Life at Thomas Jefferson's Poplar Forest*. Charlottesville: University Press of Virginia.

Heidtke, Kenan. 1992. "Jamaican Red Clay Pipes." MA thesis, Texas A&M University, College Station.

Heighton, Robert F., and Kathleen A. Deagan. 1971. "A New Formula for Dating Kaolin Clay Pipestems." *Conference on Historic Site Archaeology Papers* 6: 220–29.

Henderson, Michael, and Don Walker. 2012. "The Art of Medicine: Smoking May Seriously Affect Our Skeleton." *Lancet* 379(9818): 796–97.

Hennepin, Father Louis. 1922. "Account of the Discovery of the River Mississippi and the Adjacent Country." In *The Journeys of Réné Robert Cavelier, Sieur de La Salle*, vol. 1, edited by I. J. Cox, 66–87. New York: Allerton Book Co.

Hessler, Peter. 2011. *Country Driving: A Chinese Road Trip*. New York: Harper Perennial.

Higgins, David A. 1981. "Surrey Clay Tobacco Pipes." In *The Archaeology of the Clay Tobacco Pipe: Pipes and Kilns in the London Region*, vol. 6, edited by P. Davey, 189–293. BAR International Series 97. Oxford: British Archaeological Reports.

Hill, Marilynn Wood. 1993. *Their Sisters' Keepers: Prostitution in New York City, 1830–1870*. Berkeley: University of California Press.

Historic Jamestown. 2007. "400-Year-Old Seeds Discovered in Jamestown Well Reflect Colonial Survival Efforts." http://www.historicjamestowne.org/news/tobacco_seed.php.

Holderness, B. A. 1976. *Pre-Industrial England: Economy and Society, 1500–1750*. London: J. M. Dent and Sons.

Horn, James. 1994. *Adapting to a New World: English Society in the Seventeenth-Century Chesapeake*. Chapel Hill: University of North Carolina Press.

Houghton, J. (1692–1694) 1727–1728. *Husbandry and Trade Improved*. London: Woodman and Lyon. Microfilm. Sterling Evans Library, Texas A&M University, College Station.

Hughs, Daniel. 2012. "A Case of Multiple Identities in La Florida: A Statistical Approach to Nascent Cosmopolitanism." *Historical Archaeology* 46(1): 8–27.

Hurry, Silas D., and Robert W. Keeler. 1991. "A Descriptive Analysis of the White Clay Tobacco Pipes from the St. John's Site in St. Mary's City, Maryland." In *The Archaeology of the Clay Tobacco Pipe: Chesapeake Bay*, vol. 12, edited by P. Davey and D. J. Pogue, 37–71. BAR International Series 566. Oxford: British Archaeological Reports.

Jackson, Reginald G., and Roger H. Price. 1974. *Bristol Clay Pipes: A Study of Makers and Their Marks*. Research Monograph 1. Bristol, U.K.: Bristol City Museum.

Jamaica Public Archives. 1679–1686. *Probate Inventories*, Vol. 2. Microfilm. Department of Anthropology, Texas A&M University, College Station.

———. 1686–1694. *Probate Inventories*, Vol. 2. Microfilm. Department of Anthropology, Texas A&M University, College Station.

James I. (1604) 1672. "A Counterblaste to Tobacco." In *Two Broad-Sides against Tobacco*. London: J. Hancock. Manuscript, George Arents Collection, New York Public Library.

Jamieson, Ross W. 1995. "Material Culture and Social Death: African-American Burial Practices." *Historical Archaeology* 29(4): 39–58.

Jankowiak, William and Dan Bradburd. 1996. "Using Drug Foods to Capture and Enhance Labor Performance: A Cross-Cultural Perspective." *Current Anthropology* 37 (4): 717–720.

Joseph, J. W. 2004. "Resistance and Compliance: CRM and the Archaeology of the African Diaspora." *Historical Archaeology* 38(1): 18–31.

Karshner, M. 1979. "The Tobacco Clay Pipe Industry in Norwich." In *The Archaeology of the Clay Tobacco Pipe, Britain: The Midlands and Eastern England*, vol. 1, edited by P. Davey, 295–352. BAR British Series 63. Oxford: British Archaeological Reports.

Kelley, Jennifer O., and J. Lawrence Angel. 1981. "The Armor and Drummond-Harris Sites, Governor's Land, Virginia." Unpublished report to Alain Outlaw, Virginia Landmarks Historical Commission's Research Center for Archaeology, Williamsburg.

Kelso, William. 2011. "James Fort, Lost and Found." *Colonial Williamsburg Journal* (Summer): 5–12.

Ketz, K. Anne, Elizabeth J. Abel, and Andrew J. Schmidt. 2005. "Public Image and Private Reality: An Analysis of Differentiation in a Nineteenth-Century St. Paul Bordello." *Historical Archaeology* 39(1): 74–88.

Key, Joseph Patrick. 2002. "The Calumet and the Cross: Religious Encounters in the Lower Mississippi Valley." *Arkansas Historical Quarterly* 61(2): 152–68.

King, Julia A. 1996. "The Patuxent Site." In *Living and Dying on the 17th Century Patuxent Frontier*, edited by J. A. King and D. H. Ubelaker, 15–46. Crownsville: Maryland Historical Trust Press.

———. 1997. "Tobacco, Innovation, and Economic Persistence in Nineteenth-Century Southern Maryland." *Agricultural History* 71(2): 207–36.

———. 2007. "Still Life with Tobacco: The Archaeological Uses of Dutch Art." *Historical Archaeology* 41(1): 6–22.

King, Julia A., and Douglas H. Ubelaker. 1996. "Living and Dying on the 17th Century Patuxent Frontier." In *Living and Dying on the 17th Century Patuxent Frontier*, edited by J. A. King and D. H. Ubelaker, 105–21. Crownsville: Maryland Historical Trust Press.

Kiser, Taft. 2013. "Open Season on History." *New York Times*, August 2.

Klein, Richard. 1993. *Cigarettes Are Sublime*. Durham: Duke University Press.

Kulikoff, Allan. 1986. *Tobacco and Slaves: The Development of Southern Cultures in the Chesapeake, 1680–1800*. Chapel Hill: University of North Carolina Press.

Kümin, Beat. 2007. *Drinking Matters: Public Houses and Social Exchange in Early Modern Central Europe*. Houndmills, Basingstoke, Hampshire, U.K.: Palgrave Macmillan.

Lawrence, Susan. 2003. "Exporting Culture: Archaeology and the Nineteenth-Century British Empire." *Historical Archaeology* 37(1): 20–33.

Lemaux, Peggy G. 2008. "Genetically Engineered Plants and Foods: A Scientist's Analysis of the Issues (Part I)." *Annual Review of Plant Biology* 59: 771–812.

Limerick, Patricia. 1987. *The Legacy of Conquest: The Unbroken Past of the American West*. New York: W. W. Norton.

Lowe, Richard. (1663–1674) 1938. *The Diary of Richard Lowe of Ashton-in-Makerfield, Lancashire 1663–1674*. Edited by W. Sachse. New Haven: Yale University Press.

Lucas, Gavin. 2006. "Historical Archaeology and Time." In *The Cambridge Companion to Historical Archaeology*, edited by D. Hicks and M. C. Beaudry, 34–47. Cambridge: Cambridge University Press.

Lukenbach, Al, and Taft Kiser. 2006. "Seventeenth-Century Tobacco Pipe Manufacturing in the Chesapeake Region: A Preliminary Delineation of Markers and Their Styles." In *Ceramics in America 2006*, edited by R. Hunter, 160–77. Hanover, N.H.: University Press of New England.

Lukezic, Craig. 1990. "Soils and Settlement Location in 18th Century Colonial Tidewater Virginia." *Historical Archaeology* 24(1): 1–17.

Lyng, Stephen. 2005. "Edgework and the Risk-Taking Experience." In *Edgework: The Sociology of Risk-Taking*, edited by S. Lyng, 3–14. New York: Routledge.

MacInnes, C. M. 1926. *The Early English Tobacco Trade*. London: Kegan Paul.

Mackenzie, Compton. 1958. *Sublime Tobacco*. New York: Macmillan.

Majesties Counseil for Virginia. 1620. *A Declaration of the State of the Colonie and Affaires in Virginia with the Names of Adventurors, and Summes Adventured in That Action* (June 22). Virtual Jamestown Project.

Mancall, Peter C. 2004. "Tales Tobacco Told in Sixteenth-Century Europe." *Environmental History* 9(4): 648–78.

Mann, Rob. 2004. "Smokescreens: Tobacco, Pipes, and the Transformational Power of Fur Trade Rituals." In *Smoking and Culture: The Archaeology of Tobacco Pipes in Eastern North America*, edited by S. Rafferty and R. Mann, 165–83. Knoxville: University of Tennessee Press.

Mansfield, V. 1963. "Women Clay Pipe Smokers." *Colchester Archaeological Group Quarterly Bulletin* 6: 30–32.

Maquet, Jacques. 1988. *The Aesthetic Experience: An Anthropologist Looks at the Visual Arts*. New Haven: Yale University Press.

Margolis, Stacey. 2002. "Addiction and the Ends of Desire." In *High Anxieties: Cultural Studies in Addiction*, edited by J. F. Brodie and M. Redfield, 19–37. Berkeley: University of California Press.

Markell, Ann B. 1994. "Solid Statements: Architecture, Manufacturing, and Social Change in Seventeenth-Century Virginia." In *Historical Archaeology of the Chesapeake*, edited by P. A. Shackel and B. J. Little, 51–64. Washington, D.C.: Smithsonian Institution Press.

Martin, Samuel. 1785. *An Essay on Plantership*. Antigua: Robert Mearns.

Mauss, Marcel. 1954. *The Gift: Forms and Functions of Exchange in Archaic Societies.* London: Cohen and West.

McCusker, John J. 1997. *Essays in the Economic History of the Atlantic World.* New York: Routledge.

McCusker, John J., and Russell R. Menard. 1991. *The Economy of British America, 1607–1789.* Chapel Hill: Institute of Early American History and Culture, University of North Carolina Press.

McGrath, Patrick. 1952. *Records Relating to the Society of Merchant Venturers of the City of Bristol in the Seventeenth Century.* Vol. 17. Bristol, U.K.: Bristol Record Society's Publications.

———. 1975. *Merchants and Merchandise in Seventeenth-Century Bristol.* Bristol, U.K.: Society of Merchant Venturers of the City of Bristol.

McKivigan, John R., and Thomas J. Robertson. 1996. "The Irish American Worker in Transition, 1877–1914: New York City as a Test Case." In *The New York Irish*, edited by R. H. Baylor and T. J. Meagher, 301–20. Baltimore: Johns Hopkins Press.

Menard, Russell R. 1976. "A Note on Chesapeake Tobacco Prices, 1618–1660." *Virginia Magazine of History and Biography* 84(4): 401–10.

———. 1977. "From Servants to Slaves: The Transformation of the Chesapeake Labor System." *Southern Studies* 16(4): 355–90.

———. 1980. "The Tobacco Industry in the Chesapeake Colonies, 1617–1730. An Interpretation." *Research in Economic History* 5: 107–77.

———. 2007. "Plantation Empire: How Sugar and Tobacco Planters Built Their Industries and Raised an Empire." *Agricultural History* 81(3): 309–32.

Meyer, Michael D., Erica S. Gibson, and Julia G. Costello. 2005. "City of Angels, City of Sin: Archaeology in the Los Angeles Red-Light District, ca. 1900." *Historical Archaeology* 39(1): 107–25.

Middleton, Arthur Pierce. 1953. *Tobacco Coast: A Maritime History of Chesapeake Bay in the Colonial Era.* Newport News, Va.: Mariners' Museum.

Miller, Henry M. 1994. "The Country's House Site: An Archaeological Study of a Seventeenth-Century Domestic Landscape." In *Historical Archaeology of the Chesapeake*, edited by P. A. Shackel and B. J. Little, 65–83. Washington, D.C.: Smithsonian Institution Press.

Minchinton, Walter E. 1969. "Introduction." In *The Growth of English Trade in the Seventeenth and Eighteenth Centuries*, edited by W. E. Minchinton, 1–61. London: Methuen.

Mintz, Sidney W. 1985. *Sweetness and Power: The Place of Sugar in Modern History.* New York: Viking Penguin.

———. 1996. *Tasting Food, Tasting Freedom: Excursions into Eating, Culture, and the Past.* Boston, Mass.: Beacon Press.

Mitchell, Vivienne. 1983. "The History of Nominy Plantation with Emphasis on the

Clay Tobacco Pipes." In *Historic Clay Tobacco Pipe Studies*, vol. 2, edited by B. Sudbury, 1–38. Ponca City, Okla.: Byron Sudbury.

Monardes, Nicolas. (1577) 1925. *Joyfull Newes Out of the Newe Founde World*. Vol. 1. Translated by J. Frampton. London: Constablend.

Monroe, Cameron, and Seth Mallios. 2004. "A Seventeenth-Century Colonial Cottage Industry: New Evidence and a Dating Formula for Colono Tobacco Pipes in the Chesapeake." *Historical Archaeology* 38(2): 68–82.

Morgan, Philip D. 1998. *Slave Counterpoint: Black Culture in the Eighteenth-Century Chesapeake and Lowcountry*. Omohundro Institute of Early American History and Culture, Williamsburg, Virginia. Charlotte: University of North Carolina Press.

Mouer, L. Daniel. 1993. "Chesapeake Creoles: The Creation of Folk Culture in Colonial Virginia." In *The Archaeology of 17th-Century Virginia*, edited by T. R. Reinhart and D. J. Pogue, 105–66. Richmond, Va.: Dietz Press.

Mouer, L. Daniel, Mary Ellen N. Hodges, Stephen R. Potter, Susan L. Henry Renaud, Ivor Noël Hume, Dennis J. Pogue, Martha W. McCartney, and Thomas E. Davidson. 1999. "Colonoware Pottery, Chesapeake Pipes, and 'Uncritical Assumptions.'" In *"I, Too, Am America": Archaeological Studies of African-American Life*, edited by T. A. Singleton, 83–115. Charlottesville: University Press of Virginia.

Mrozowski, Stephen A. 1993. "The Dialectics of a Historical Archaeology in a Post-Processual World." *Historical Archaeology* 27(2): 106–11.

———. 2006. *The Archaeology of Class in Urban America*. Cambridge: Cambridge University Press.

Mrozowski, Stephen A., Grace H. Ziesing, and Mary C. Beaudry. 1996. *Living on the Boott: Historical Archaeology at the Boott Mills Boardinghouses, Lowell, Massachusetts*. Amherst: University of Massachusetts Press.

Mullins, Paul R. 1999. *Race and Affluence: An Archaeology of African America and Consumer Culture*. New York: Kluwer Academic/Plenum Publishers.

———. 2011. *The Archaeology of Consumer Culture*. Gainesville: University Press of Florida.

Nash, Robert C. 1999. "The Organization of Trade and Finance in the British Atlantic Economy, 1600–1830." In *The Atlantic Economy during the Seventeenth and Eighteenth Centuries: Organization, Operation, Practice, and Personnel*, edited by P. A. Coclanis, 95–151. Columbia: University of South Carolina Press.

Nassaney, Michael S. 2004. "Men and Women, Pipes and Power in Native New England." In *Smoking and Culture: The Archaeology of Tobacco Pipes in Eastern North America*, edited by S. Rafferty and R. Mann, 125–41. Knoxville: University of Tennessee Press.

Nassaney, Michael S., and Eric S. Johnson. 2000. "The Contributions of Material

Objects to Ethnohistory in Native North America." In *Interpretations of Native North American Life*, edited by M. S. Nassaney and E. S. Johnson, 1–30. Gainesville: University Press of Florida.

Náter, Laura. 1999. "The Spanish Empire and Cuban Tobacco during the Seventeenth and Eighteenth Centuries." In *The Atlantic Economy during the Seventeenth and Eighteenth Centuries: Organization, Operation, Practice, and Personnel*, edited by P. A. Coclanis, 252–76. Columbia: University of South Carolina Press.

Nöel Hume, Ivor. 1969. *A Guide to Artifacts of Colonial America*. New York: Alfred Knopf.

———. 1982. *Martin's Hundred*. New York: Alfred A. Knopf.

———. 1994. *The Virginal Adventure: Roanoke to James Towne: An Archaeological and Historical Odyssey*. New York: Alfred A. Knopf.

Norman, Neil L. 2012. "From the Shadow of an Atlantic Citadel: An Archaeology of the Huedan Countryside." In *Power and Landscape in Atlantic West Africa: Archaeological Perspectives*, edited by J. Cameron Monroe and A. Ogundiran, 142–68. Cambridge: Cambridge University Press.

O'Brien, Patrick. 1982. "European Economic Development: The Contribution of the Periphery." *Economic History Review* 35: 1–18.

Office of the Exchequer. 1682. *London and Bristol Port Books, Series E/190*. London, U.K.: National Archives.

———. 1694–1695. *London and Bristol Port Books, Series E/190*. London, U.K.: National Archives.

Orser, Charles E. 1996. *Images of the Recent Past: Readings in Historical Archaeology*. Walnut Creek, Calif.: AltaMira Press.

Oswald, Adrian. 1959. "A Case of Transatlantic Deduction." *Antiques* 76: 59–61.

———. 1975. *Clay Pipes for the Archaeologist*. BAR British Series 14. Oxford: British Archaeological Reports.

Pagan, John Ruston. 1979. "Growth of the Tobacco Trade between London and Virginia, 1614–40." *Guildhall Studies in London History* 3: 248–62.

Patten, John. 1978. *English Towns: 1500–1700*. Kent, U.K.: William Dawson and Sons.

Pawson, Michael, and David Buisseret. 2000. *Port Royal, Jamaica*. Oxford: Oxford University Press.

Peacey, Allan A. 1996. *The Archaeology of the Clay Tobacco Pipe, Vol. XIV: The Development of the Clay Tobacco Pipe Kiln in the British Isles*. Edited by P. Davey. BAR British Series 246. Oxford: British Archaeological Reports.

Peiss, Kathy. 1986. *Cheap Amusements: Working Women and Leisure in Turn-of-the-Century New York*. Philadelphia: Temple University Press.

Peña, Elizabeth S., and Jacqueline Denmon. 2000. "The Social Organization of a Boardinghouse: Archaeological Evidence from the Buffalo Waterfront." *Historical Archaeology* 34(1): 79–96.

Pendery, Steven R. 1992. "Consumer Behavior in Colonial Charlestown, Massachusetts, 1630–1760." *Historical Archeology* 26(3): 52–72.

Penn, W. A. 1901. *The Soverane Herbe: A History of Tobacco.* London: Grant Richards.

Pestana, Carla. 2004. *The English Atlantic in an Age of Revolution, 1640–1661.* Cambridge, Mass.: Harvard University Press.

Phung, Thao T., Julia King, and Douglas H. Ubelaker. 2009. "Alcohol, Tobacco,
and Excessive Animal Protein: The Question of an Adequate Diet in the Seventeenth-Century Chesapeake." *Historical Archaeology* 43(2): 61–82.

Poling, Jim. 2012. *Smoke Signals: The Native Takeback of North America's Tobacco
Industry.* Toronto: Dundurn Press.

Pope, Peter E. 2004. *Fish into Wine: The Newfoundland Plantation in the Seventeenth
Century.* Chapel Hill: University of North Carolina Press.

Price, David A. 2003. *Love and Hate in Jamestown: John Smith, Pocahontas, and the
Start of a New Nation.* New York: Vintage Books.

Price, Jacob M. 1964. "The Economic Growth of the Chesapeake and the European
Market, 1697–1775." *Journal of Economic History* 24(4): 496–511.

———. 1978. "Colonial Trade and British Economic Development, 1660–1775." *Lex
et Scientia: The International Journal of Law and Science* 14: 101–26.

Price, Jacob M., and Paul G. E. Clemens. 1987. "A Revolution of Scale in Overseas
Trade: British Firms in the Chesapeake Trade, 1665–1775." *Journal of Economic
History* 47(1): 1–43.

Pullins, Stevan C., Joe B. Jones, John R. Underwood, Kimberly A. Ettinger, and David W. Lewes. 2003. "Southall's Quarter: Archaeology at an Eighteenth-Century
Slave Quarter in James City County." Report Prepared for the Virginia Department of Transportation. Williamsburg: William and Mary Center for Archaeological Research.

Rafferty, Sean M. 2001. "They Pass Their Lives in Smoke, and at Death, Fall into the
Fire: Smoking Pipes and Mortuary Ritual during the Early Woodland Period."
PhD dissertation, Binghamton University, State University of New York.

———. 2004. "'They Pass Their Lives in Smoke, and at Death Fall into the Fire':
Smoking Pipes and Mortuary Ritual during the Early Woodland Period." In
Smoking and Culture: The Archaeology of Tobacco Pipes in Eastern North America,
edited by S. Rafferty and R. Mann, 1–41. Knoxville: University of Tennessee
Press.

Rafferty, Sean M., and Rob Mann. 2004. "Introduction: Smoking Pipes and Culture." In *Smoking and Culture: The Archaeology of Tobacco Pipes in Eastern North
America,* edited by S. Rafferty and R. Mann, xi–xx. Knoxville: University of Tennessee Press.

Ramsay, George D. 1957. *English Overseas Trade during the Centuries of Emergence.* London: Macmillan.

Ranzetta, Kirk E. 2005. "The Myth of Agricultural Complacency: Tobacco Barns of St. Mary's County, Maryland, 1790–1890." *Perspectives in Vernacular Architecture: Building Environments* 10: 81–96.

Rapún, Nicolas Jose. 1764. "Instruccion General de el Cultivo de Tavacos." Unpublished MS.

Reay, Barry. 1985. "Introduction: Popular Culture in Early Modern England." In *Popular Culture in Seventeenth-Century England*, edited by B. Reay, 1–30. New York: St. Martin's Press.

Reckner, Paul E. 2001. "Negotiating Patriotism at the Five Points: Clay Tobacco Pipes and the Patriotic Imagery among Trade Unionists and Nativists in a Nineteenth-Century New York Neighborhood." *Historical Archaeology* 35(3): 103–14.

———. 2004. "Home Rulers, Red Hands, and Radical Journalists: Clay Pipes and the Negotiation of Working-Class Irish/Irish American Identity in Late-Nineteenth-Century Paterson, New Jersey." In *Smoking and Culture: The Archaeology of Tobacco Pipes in Eastern North America*, edited by S. Rafferty and R. Mann, 241–71. Knoxville: University of Tennessee Press.

Reckner, Paul, and Stephen A. Brighton. 1999. "'Free from All Vicious Habits': Archaeological Perspectives on Class Conflict and the Rhetoric of Temperance." *Historical Archaeology* 33(1): 63–86.

Reith, Gerda. 2004. "Consumption and Its Discontents: Addiction, Identity and the Problems of Freedom." *British Journal of Sociology* 55(2): 283–300.

Renk, Kathleen J. 1999. *Caribbean Shadows and Victorian Ghosts: Women's Writing and Decolonization.* Charlottesville: University of Virginia Press.

Rich, Barnaby. (1615) 1937. "The Honestie of This Age." In *Tobacco: Its History Illustrated by the Books, Manuscripts and Engravings in the Library of George Arents, Jr.*, vol. 1, 537–38. New York: Rosenbach.

Richards, Thomas, Catherine M. Bennett, and Harry Webber. 2012. "A Post-Contact Aboriginal Mortuary Tree from Southwestern Victoria, Australia." *Journal of Field Archaeology* 37(1): 62–72.

Robert, Joseph C. 1967. *The Story of Tobacco in America.* Chapel Hill: University of North Carolina Press.

Rotman, Deborah. 2009. *Historical Archaeology of Gendered Lives.* New York: Springer.

Rublowsky, John. 1974. *The Stoned Age: A History of Drugs in America.* New York: G. P. Putnam's Sons.

Rudy, Jarrett. 2005. *The Freedom to Smoke: Tobacco Consumption and Identity.* Kingston, Ontario: McGill-Queen's University Press.

Russell, Matthew A. 2011. "Encounters at *tamal-huye*: An Archaeology of Intercultural Engagement in Sixteenth-Century Northern California." PhD dissertation, University of California, Berkeley.

Russo, Jean B., and J. Elliott Russo. 2012. *Planting an Empire: The Early Chesapeake in British North America*. Baltimore: Johns Hopkins University Press.

Scammell, G. V. 1989. *European Overseas Expansion, C. 1400–1715*. London: Unwin Hyman.

Schablitsky, Julie M. 2007. "Western Boomtowns: The Lost Episodes." In *Box Office Archaeology: Refining Hollywood's Portrayals of the Past*, edited by J. M. Schablitsky, 179–99. Walnut Creek, Calif.: Left Coast Press.

Schama, Simon. 1987. *The Embarrassment of Riches: An Interpretation of Dutch Culture in the Golden Age*. Los Angeles: University of California Press.

Scott, Douglas D., and Clyde Collins Snow. 1991. "Archaeology and Forensic Anthropology of the Human Remains from the Reno Retreat Crossing." In *Papers on Little Bighorn Battlefield Archaeology: The Equipment Dump, Marker 7 and the Reno Crossing*, edited by D. Scott, 207–36. Reprints in Anthropology, 42. Lincoln, Nebr.: J and L Reprint Co.

Scott, Douglas D., and P. Willey. 1997. "Little Bighorn: Human Remains from the Custer National Cemetery." In *Remembrance: Archaeology and Death*, edited by D. A. Poirier and N. F. Bellantoni, 155–71. Westport, Conn.: Bergin and Garvey.

Scott, Douglas D., P. Willey, and Melissa A. Connor. 1998. *They Died with Custer: Soldiers' Bones from the Battle of Little Bighorn*. Norman: University of Oklahoma Press.

Seifert, Donna J. 1991. "Within Site of the White House: The Archaeology of Working." *Historical Archaeology* 25(4): 82–108.

Seifert, Donna J., and Joseph Balicki. 2005. "Mary Ann Hall's House." *Historical Archaeology* 39(1): 59–73.

Shackel, Paul A., and Barbara J. Little. 1994. "Archaeological Perspectives: An Overview of the Chesapeake Region." In *Historical Archaeology of the Chesapeake*, edited by P. A. Shackel and B. J. Little, 1–15. Washington, D.C.: Smithsonian Institution Press.

Shammas, Carole. 1990. *The Preindustrial Consumer in England and America*. Oxford: Clarendon Press.

———. 2000. "The Revolutionary Impact of European Demand for Tropical Goods." In *The Early Modern Atlantic Economy*, edited by J. J. McCusker and K. Morgan, 163–85. Cambridge: Cambridge University Press.

———. 2005. "America, the Atlantic, and Global Consumer Demand, 1500–1800." *Organization of American Historians (OAH) Magazine of History* 19(1): 59–64.

Shennan, Stephen. 1989. "Introduction: Archaeological Approaches to Cultural Identity." In *Archaeological Approaches to Cultural Identity*, edited by S. Shennan, 1–32. London: Unwin Hyman.

Sheridan, Richard. 1973. *Sugar and Slavery: An Economic History of the British West Indies, 1623–1775*. Baltimore: Johns Hopkins University Press.

Sherratt, Andrew. 2007. "Introduction: Peculiar Substances." In *Consuming Habits: Drugs in History and Anthropology*, edited by J. Goodman, A. Sherratt, and P. E. Lovejoy, 1–10. New York: Routledge.

Silliman, Stephen W., and Thomas A. Witt. 2010. "The Complexities of Consumption: Eastern Pequot Cultural Economics in Eighteenth-Century New England." *Historical Archaeology* 44(4): 46–68.

Smith, Colin. 2002. "The Wholesale and Retail Markets of London, 1660–1840." *Economic History Review* 56(1): 31–50.

Smith, Frederick H. 2005. *Caribbean Rum: A Social and Economic History*. Gainesville: University Press of Florida.

———. 2008. *The Archaeology of Alcohol and Drinking*. Gainesville: University Press of Florida.

South, Stanley. 1977. *Method and Theory in Historical Archaeology*. New York: Academic Press.

———. 1978. "Pattern Recognition in Historical Archaeology." *American Antiquity* 43(2): 223–30.

Springer, James Warren. 1981. "An Ethnohistoric Study of the Smoking Complex in Eastern North America." *Ethnohistory* 28(3): 217–35.

Spude, Catherine Holder. 2005. "Brothels and Saloons: An Archaeology of Gender in the American West." *Historical Archaeology* 39(1): 89–106.

Stein, Gil. 1999. *Rethinking World-Systems*. Tucson: University of Arizona Press.

Sudbury, J. Byron. 2009. *Politics of the Fur Trade: Clay Tobacco Pipes at Fort Union Trading Post (32WI17)*. Historic Clay Tobacco Pipe Studies Research Monograph. Ponca, Okla.: Clay Pipes Press, a Division of Phytolith Press.

Taylor, S. A. G. 1965. *The Western Design: An Account of Cromwell's Expedition to the Caribbean*. Kingston: Institute of Jamaica and the Jamaica Historical Society.

Thackeray, J. Francis, Nikolaas J. van der Merwe, and T. A. van der Merwe. 2001. "Chemical Analysis of Residues from Seventeenth-Century Clay Pipes from Stratford-upon-Avon and Environs: Research in Action." *South African Journal of Science* 97(1/2): 19–21.

Thirsk, Joan. 1978. *Economic Policy and Projects: The Development of a Consumer Society in Early Modern England*. Oxford: Clarendon Press.

Trubowitz, Neal L. 2004. "Smoking Pipes: An Archaeological Measure of Native American Cultural Stability and Survival in Eastern North America, A.D. 1500–1850." In *Smoking and Culture: The Archaeology of Tobacco Pipes in Eastern North America*, edited by S. Rafferty and R. Mann, 143–64. Knoxville: University of Tennessee Press.

Tryon, Thomas. 1699. *England's Grandeur and Way to Get Wealth, or Promotion of Trade Made Easy and Lands Advanced.* London: Harrow and G. Conyers.

Turnbaugh, William A. 1975. "Tobacco, Pipes, Smoking, and Rituals among the Indians of the Northeast." *Quarterly Bulletin of the Archaeological Society of Virginia* 30(2): 59–71.

Ubelaker, Douglas H., Erica Bubniak Jones, and Abigail W. Turowski. 1996. "Skeletal Biology of the Patuxent Point Human Remains." In *Living and Dying on the 17th Century Patuxent Frontier*, edited by J. A. King and D. H. Ubelaker, 47–104. Crownsville: Maryland Historical Trust Press.

Veblen, Thorstein. 1899. *The Theory of the Leisure Class.* New York: Dover.

Vihlene, Shannon M. 2008. "Custer's Last Drag: An Examination of Tobacco Use among the Seventh Cavalry during the Nineteenth Century." MA thesis, University of Montana.

Vince, Alan, and Allan Peacey. 2006. "Pipemakers and Their Workshops: The Use of Geochemical Analysis in the Study of the Clay Tobacco Pipe Industry." In *Between Dirt and Discussion: Methods, Methodology and Interpretation in Historical Archaeology*, edited by S. Archer and K. Bartoy, 11–31. New York: Springer.

von Gernet, Alexander. 1995. "Nicotine Dreams: The Prehistory and Early History of Tobacco in Eastern North America." In *Consuming Habits: Drugs in History and Anthropology*, edited by J. Goodman, P. E. Lovejoy, and A. Sherratt, 67–87. London: Routledge.

Walker, Iain C. 1971. "Some Notes on the Westminster and London Tobacco-Pipe Makers' Guild." *Transactions of the London and Middlesex Archaeological Society* 23: 78–89.

———. 1977. *Clay Tobacco Pipes with a Particular Reference to the Bristol Industry.* History and Archaeology, vols. 11a–11d. Ottawa: Parks Canada.

———. 1983. "Nineteenth-Century Clay Pipes in Canada." In *The Archaeology of the Clay Tobacco Pipe, Vol. VIII: America*, edited by P. Davey, 1–87. BAR International Series 175. Oxford: British Archaeological Reports.

Wallerstein, Immanuel. 1974. *The Modern World System.* New York: Academic Press.

———. 1980. *The Modern World System II: Mercantilism and the Consolidation of the European World-Economy, 1600–1750.* New York: Academic Press.

Walsh, Lorena S. 1999. "Summing the Parts: Implications for Estimating Chesapeake Output and Income Subregionally." *William and Mary Quarterly* 56(1): 53–94.

———. 2001. *From Calabar to Carter's Grove: A History of a Virginia Slave Community.* Charlottesville: University Press of Virginia.

———. 2010. *Motives of Honor, Pleasure, and Profit: Plantation Management in the Colonial Chesapeake, 1607–1763.* Chapel Hill: North Carolina University Press.

———. 2011. "Boom-and-Bust Cycles in Chesapeake History." *William and Mary Quarterly* 68(3): 387–92.

Ward, N. Edward. 1927. *The London Spy: The Vanities and Vices of the Town Exposed to View*. Edited by A. Hayward. London: Cassell.

———. 1933. *Five Travel Scripts Commonly Attributed to Edward Ward*. New York: Columbia University Press.

Weatherill, Lorna. 1988. *Consumer Behavior and Material Culture in Britain, 1660–1760*. London: Routledge.

White, Bruce M. 1982. "'Give Us a Little Milk': The Social and Cultural Meanings of Gift Giving in the Lake Superior Fur Trade." *Minnesota History* 48(2): 60–71.

White, Carolyn L., ed. 2009. *The Materiality of Individuality: Archaeological Studies of Individual Lives*. New York: Springer.

Wilentz, Sean. 1984. "Against Exceptionalism: Class Consciousness and the American Labor Movement, 1790–1920." *International Labor and Working-Class History* 26: 1–24.

Willey, P. 1997. *Osteological Analysis of Human Skeletons Excavated from the Custer National Cemetery*. Technical Report No. 50. Lincoln: National Park Service, Midwest Archaeological Center.

Willey, P., Richard A. Glenner, and Douglas D. Scott. 1996. "Oral Health of Seventh Cavalry Troopers: Dentitions from the Custer National Cemetery." *Journal of the History of Dentistry* 44(1): 3–14.

Willey P., and Douglas D. Scott. 1999. "Who's Buried in Custer's Grave?" *Journal of Forensic Sciences* 44(3): 656–65.

Wilson, Charles. 1984. *England's Apprenticeship, 1603–1763*. London: Longman.

Winter, Joseph C. 2000a. "Botanical Descriptions of the North American Tobacco Species." In *Tobacco Use by Native North Americans: Sacred Smoke and Silent Killer*, edited by J. Winter, 87–127. Norman: University of Oklahoma Press.

———. 2000b. "Food of the Gods: Biochemistry, Addiction, and the Development of Native American Tobacco Use." In *Tobacco Use by Native North Americans: Sacred Smoke and Silent Killer*, edited by J. Winter, 305–28. Norman: University of Oklahoma Press.

———. 2000c. "From Earth Mother to Snake Woman: The Role of Tobacco in the Evolution of Native American Religious Organization." In *Tobacco Use by Native North Americans: Sacred Smoke and Silent Killer*, edited by J. Winter, 265–304. Norman: University of Oklahoma Press.

Winter, Joseph C., Glenn W. Solomon, Robert F. Hill, Christina M. Pego, and Suzanne E. Victoria. 2000. "Native Americans and Tobacco: Deer Person's Gift or Columbus's Curse?" In *Tobacco Use by Native North Americans: Sacred Smoke and Silent Killer*, edited by J. Winter, 353–81. Norman: University of Oklahoma Press.

Withington, Phil. 2011. "Intoxicants and Society in Early Modern England." *Historical Journal* 54(3): 631–57.

Wolf, Eric. 1982. *Europe and the People without History*. Berkeley: University of California Press.

Woodward, Donald. 1994. "The Determination of Wage Rates in the Early Modern North of England." *Economic History Review* 47(1): 22–43.

Wurst, LouAnn. 2006. "A Class All Its Own: Explorations of Class Formation and Conflict." In *Historical Archaeology*, edited by M. Hall and S. W. Silliman, 190–206. Malden, Mass.: Blackwell Press.

Yamin, Rebecca. 1997. "New York's Mythic Slum: Digging Lower Manhattan's Infamous Five Points." *Archaeology* 50(2): 45–53.

———. 2001. "Introduction: Becoming New York: The Five Points Neighborhood." *Historical Archaeology* 35(3): 1–5.

Zahedieh, Nuala. 1986. "Trade, Plunder and Economic Development in Early English Jamaica, 1655–89." *Economic History Review* 39(2): 205–22.

———. 1994. "London and the Colonial Consumer in the Late Seventeenth Century." *Economic History Review* 47(2): 239–61.

Index

Puritan attitudes toward tobacco and
smoking, 24

"Quality control" of pipe making, 40, 43
Quarter Site, 81
Quids, 19

Radiocarbon dating, 59–60
Rafferty, Sean, 2, 3, 59, 68
Raleigh, Sir Walter, 20, 51, 52, 76
Ranzetta, Kirk, 34
Rations, tobacco as, 96, 97–98
Rebellion and resistance, smoking as,
133–34
Reckner, Paul, 2, 84, 87, 89–91
Red clay pipes, 60–64, 80–81, 99, 100, 110,
123
Redfield, Marc, 4
"Red Hand of Ulster" motifs, 91
Red stone (catlinite) pipe bowls, 67
Re-export trade, 9, 12, 15, 21–22, 30, 33
Refuse disposal, patterns of, 113–15
Reintroduction of tobacco to Native
Americans, 67–69, 105
Rembrandt van Rijn, 60
Renoir, Pierre-Auguste, 48
Respectability, public smoking and
women's, 86, 92–95, 102–3
Rhode Island cemeteries, 69, 70
RI-1000, 69, 70
Rich, Barnaby, 124
Rich Neck Plantation, Virginia, 63
Right-angle elbow stone pipes, 71–72
Ritualized gift exchanges, 71–75, 103, 105
Ritual use of tobacco pipes, 19, 68–69;
Calumet Ceremony, 72–75, 105
Riverfront Augusta Site, 47
Robert, Joseph C., 98
Rockingham Ware, 6
Rolfe, John, 27, 76
Rolled tobacco, 19, 20, 105, 132
Rouletting, 46, 120
Ryckaert, David, 57

Sabbath, smoking on, 24
Saloons and brothels, 99–103, 104
Savage, Elizabeth, 56
Schama, Simon, 58
Scorsese, Martin, 88
Scottish tobacco pipes, 47, 121
"Sea foam" pipes. See Meerschaum pipes
Seifert, Donna, 101–2
Semiperipheries, 9–10, 22
Sepiolite, 99
Servants, indentured. See Indentured
servitude
Seventh Cavalry, tobacco use by, 95–98
Sexuality, smoking and women's, 58,
94
Shakespeare, William, 60
Shammas, Carole, 11, 126
Shamrock and harp motifs, 91
Shape changes in bowl styles, 45, 117, 118
Shipping records, evidence of clay to-
bacco pipes in, 39, 43–44, 120–23
Short-stemmed pipes. See "Cutties"
Silica, 40
Size changes in bowl styles, 45, 117, 118
Skeletal remains, evidence of tobacco
use in, 78–80, 96–98
Slave-based economy seen as necessity,
34–35
Slave labor, transition to, 34–36, 38
Slave quarters, excavations at, 82–83
Slavery. See Enslaved labor, adoption of
Smith, Frederick, 6, 132
Smoking Age, The (Braithwait), 54
Smoking and Culture (Rafferty and
Mann, eds.), 68
"Smoking complex" of native North
Americans, 67
Smoking paraphernalia, 50, 52, 122–23
Snuff, 20, 50
Snuff boxes, 50
Soapstone elbow pipe, 71–72
Sociability and tobacco consumption, 4,
23–24, 129–30

Tobacco use, early accounts of, 19–20
Tracts as documentary evidence, 2, 19, 39,
 53
Transculturation. *See* Reintroduction of
 tobacco
Trubowitz, Neal, 68–69
Tubercular skeletal lesions, 69–70
Tudor rose design, 46, 120
"Turk's Head" pipe, 47–48, 121
Typologies, 117–21

Ubelaker, Douglas, 78, 79
Underwater images, *111*, *112*
University of California, Davis, Archaeom-
 etry Laboratory, 59–60
Unsmoked clay pipes, recovery of, *112*, 119
Updraft kilns, 40, *41*
U.S. Cavalry, tobacco use by, 95–98

van der Merwe, Nikolaas J., 60
van der Merwe, T. A., 60
Veblen, Thorstein, 13
Verbraack, Captain Nicholas, 122
Vespucci, Amerigo, 19
Vihlene, Shannon, 95, 96, 97, 98
Virginia and Maryland tobacco economies.
 See Chesapeake, the
Virginia City saloon site studies, 49, 50, 58,
 99–100
Virginia Company. *See* Jamestown
"Voiceless" peoples, tobacco as conduit to
 understanding, 3, 10–11, 103–5

Wages, pipe makers', 44
Walker, Don, 79
Walker, Iain, 45
Wall, Diana, 101
Wallerstein, Immanuel, 5, 8–9, 11, 107
Walsh, Lorena, 77, 80, 82
Ward, N. Edward, 54–55, 127
Washington, D.C., assemblages, 101–2
Wear facets, dental. *See* Dental evidence of
 tobacco use
Weatherill, Lorna, 11, 126

West, Sir Thomas, 76
West African influences in grave goods,
 82–83
West Africans' use of tobacco and pipes,
 80, 82–83
Western boomtown saloons, 99–100,
 102–3
Western Design, Cromwell's, 23
West Indian slave trade. *See* Enslaved labor,
 adoption of
White, Robert, 123
White ball clays, 40
White clay pipes, 50, 63, 68–69, 70–71,
 82–83, 99; art of making, 39–49; at
 Green Spring Plantation, 80–81; at
 Jamestown, 76–77; at Port Royal, 106,
 109–15, 117, 119–22
Willey, P., 96, 97
Winter, Joseph, 21
Withington, Phil, 3, 128–29
"Wolf 98 Tone" emblems, 91
Woman Seated Smoking a Pipe, A (Metsu),
 56, 57, 127–28
Women and smoking: in Dutch art, 54,
 56–58; Huedan, 80; in Late Victorian
 America, 91–95; literary references to,
 54–56; Narragansett, 69–70; scientific
 evidence of, 58–59, 100; Taíno, 19;
 working-class, 85–86, 93–94
Wooden pipes, 49, 65, 68, 89
Wooden stems, 71–72
Working-class identity formation: at Boott
 Mills, 84–86; among Irish Americans,
 84, 87–91
World-systems theory, 5, 8–12, 15, 25, 107
Wriothesley, Henry, 76

Yamin, Rebecca, 88
Yard 4A/4B, 113, 121
Yeardley, George, 34
Yellow-flowered tobacco species. *See N.
 rustica*

Zahedieh, Nuala, 108

GEORGIA L. FOX is professor of anthropology at California State University, Chico, where she specializes in historical archaeology, museum studies, and the conservation of archaeological materials.

THE AMERICAN EXPERIENCE IN ARCHAEOLOGICAL PERSPECTIVE
Edited by Michael S. Nassaney

The books in this series explore events, processes, settings, or institutions that were significant in the formative experience of contemporary America. Each volume frames the topic beyond an individual site and attempts to give the reader a flavor of the theoretical, methodological, and substantive issues that researchers face in their examination of that topic or theme. These books are comprehensive overviews that allow serious students and scholars to get a good sense of contemporary and past inquiries on broad themes in American history and culture.

Lightning Source UK Ltd.
Milton Keynes UK
UKHW012354210421
382416UK00001B/95